JESUS

AND  THE

KINGDOM

UNLOCKING HUMANITY'S CALLING
AND THE KINGDOM'S POWER

TOM CORNELL

JESUS AND THE KINGDOM

UNLOCKING HUMANITY'S CALLING AND THE
KINGDOM'S POWER

TOM CORNELL

SOZO PUBLISHING

Copyright © 2025 by Tom Cornell

All rights reserved.

No portion of this book may be reproduced in any form or by any means without written permission from the publisher or author, except as permitted by U.S. copyright law. First edition with updates.

Paperback ISBN: 979-8-9925380-0-7

Ebook ISBN: 979-8-9925380-1-4

Bible quotations are taken from:

The New King James Version® (NKJV). Copyright © 1982 by Thomas Nelson. Used by permission. All rights reserved.

New American Standard Bible 1995 (NASB1995). New American Standard Bible®, Copyright © 1960, 1971, 1977, 1995 by The Lockman Foundation. All Rights Reserved.

The *Holy Bible*, New Living Translation (NLT). Copyright © 1996, 2004, 2015 by Tyndale House Foundation. Used by permission of Tyndale House Publishers, Inc., Carol Stream, Illinois 60188. All rights reserved.

The Amplified Bible, Classic Edition (AMPC). Copyright © 1954, 1958, 1962, 1964, 1965, 1987 by The Lockman Foundation."

PRAISE FOR JESUS AND THE KINGDOM

Tom Cornell unveiled the understanding of your place in the Kingdom of God and what is the original purpose of your existence on earth. I believe that every Christian must read the bible with the Kingdom perspective, not a religious perspective. "For the LORD Most High is awesome, a great king over all the earth" (Psalm 47:2). This insight on the hidden kingdom residing in each of us is a perfect prescription to inject new life in Christ Jesus. As you read Jesus and the Kingdom, allow Holy Spirit to transfer to you supernatural Kingdom authority and power.

— DR. ISRAEL KIM FOUNDER AND OVERSEER APOSTLES MINISTRIES EMPOWERMENT NETWORK LIVING WATERS APOSTOLIC CENTER FEDERAL WAY, WASHINGTON

CONTENTS

Introduction	vii
1. The Need for the Kingdom	1
2. The Promise of the Kingdom	8
3. The Arrival of the King	24
4. The Way of the Kingdom	42
5. The Ethics of the Kingdom	69
6. The Throne of the Kingdom	92
7. The Life of the Kingdom	103
8. He is Risen	114
Conclusion	133
About the Author	137

INTRODUCTION
SEEING THE BIBLE THROUGH THE LENS OF JESUS AND HIS KINGDOM

If there is one truth that will transform how you understand the entire Bible, it is this: God's original intent for humanity was His Kingdom, and Jesus came to restore it. The Bible is not just a book of religious principles, moral stories, or an escape plan for heaven—it is the revelation of God's divine purpose to establish His rule on the earth through His people.

In the beginning, before sin entered the world, Eden was the picture of God's perfect rule—a place where heaven and earth were one, where man lived in complete alignment with God's will. Adam was created in God's image, given authority to rule, multiply, and subdue the earth under God's dominion. This was the original design: God and man ruling together in perfect harmony.

But when sin entered, that divine order was disrupted. The earth fell under corruption, and humanity lost its place of rulership. Yet, from Genesis onward, God's plan was never to abandon His creation but to restore what was lost. The entire Old Testament is the unfolding story of God's commitment to bringing His

Kingdom back to the earth. The prophets spoke of a coming restoration, a time when God would redeem what was desolate and reestablish His rule among men (Isaiah 61:4).

Then Jesus came, and His first message was: "The Kingdom of God is at hand" (Mark 1:15). He wasn't just talking about salvation from sin—He was announcing the restoration of God's rule on earth. This is why He taught His disciples to pray, "Your Kingdom come, Your will be done, on earth as it is in heaven" (Matthew 6:10). Jesus was reestablishing what Adam lost. His mission was to bring the reign of heaven back into the earth, and He did so through His life, His death, and His resurrection.

Many Christians live their lives only thinking about getting to heaven—but the reality is, God's plan has always been about bringing heaven to earth. Instead of an escape plan, God has a restoration plan. The call of every believer is not just to hold on until we leave, but to partner with God to see His Kingdom expand in every sphere of life.

What This Book Is About

This book is about Jesus and His Kingdom. It's about rediscovering the Gospel not just as a message of personal salvation, but as the announcement of God's reign being restored. It's about understanding the Bible through a Kingdom lens—seeing how everything in Scripture points to Jesus as King, and how His mission was to restore all things under God's original intent.

If you have ever felt like your Christian life is just about waiting for heaven, this book will awaken you to your true purpose. You were made to walk in dominion with God, to bring His Kingdom into the world around you. As you read, your perspective will shift, and you will begin to see how the Kingdom of God is not just a future reality, but a present invitation—one that calls you to live fully aligned with God's will, bringing heaven's reality into the earth today.

1

THE NEED FOR THE KINGDOM

There was a moment in history when the streets of Jerusalem erupted with cries of "Hosanna! Save us!" The people laid their cloaks on the ground and waved palm branches as a king rode into the city—not on a warhorse, but on a colt. The scene was electric, filled with expectation. A Messiah had come, but not in the way anyone had anticipated.

They cried out for salvation because they knew something was wrong. They lived under oppression, not just from Rome, but from a deeper enemy. The problem was greater than earthly rulers or kingdoms—it was spiritual. There was something in the world, something in their own hearts, that was broken. They needed more than a political revolution. **They needed a new kind of kingdom.**

To understand the significance of this moment—The Triumphal Entry—we must go back to the beginning. Before the cries of the people, before the cross, before even the law was given. We must go back to when humanity's hope was first whispered in the Garden of Eden.

Genesis, the book of beginnings, tells us that God created a good world. In the midst of that world, He planted a garden called Eden—meaning delight—a place where heaven and earth met, where God walked with man. He created humanity to thrive in relationship with Himself, to rule over creation, and to experience life without death.

This was the original Kingdom of God on earth.

It was a kingdom built on covenant—a relationship of trust, love, and obedience between God and mankind. It was a kingdom of peace, where Adam and Eve lived in harmony with their Creator. There was no suffering, no oppression, no injustice.

But something went wrong.

God had given Adam and Eve the freedom to choose, and they chose wrongly. They listened to the voice of the serpent instead of the voice of their Creator. In doing so, they separated themselves from the very source of life.

Proverbs warns, *"There is a way that seems right to a man, But its end is the way of death." (Proverbs 14:12 NKJV)*. And that was the result—death entered the world. Physical death. Spiritual death. The created order was fractured.

Mankind was now ruled by something other than God's wisdom. Instead of trusting in Yahweh, they trusted in their own understanding. And with that, sin and death took the throne.

The Kingdom of God was lost on earth.

Yet even in their failure, God made a promise. He declared that one would come from the woman—a seed who would crush the head of the serpent. This coming one would reverse what had been done. He would restore what had been lost.

But in order to crush the serpent, He would have to conquer death itself.

From that moment, the world was left waiting for this promise to be fulfilled. As history unfolded, humanity's need for this coming King became increasingly clear.

Violence, corruption, and rebellion spread. The people of the earth built cities and nations, seeking power, but all fell into disorder. The greatest kingdoms of men—Egypt, Assyria, Babylon—were marked not by peace but by oppression. Every earthly government was ultimately ruled by the same force: sin.

Instead of ruling with God, mankind sought to rule without Him.

Then God called a man—Abraham. He told him that through his seed, all nations would be blessed. The promise moved from Abraham to Isaac, then to Jacob. And then, Jacob prophesied over his son Judah:

"The scepter shall not depart from Judah... And to him shall be the obedience of the people" (Genesis 49:10 NKJV).

A king is coming.

But He does not come immediately. The people wait. Generations pass. Then, a shepherd boy from Judah is anointed as king—David. Could this be the one? He slays giants, expands Israel's borders, and is called a man after God's own heart.

But then he falls.

David's sin with Bathsheba proves that he, too, is under the power of sin. He is not the serpent-crusher. Yet, because he humbles himself before God, Yahweh makes him a promise—someone from his lineage will sit on the throne forever.

How could this be? Every king eventually dies. If death claims every ruler, then for this King to reign forever, He must conquer death itself.

But after David, Israel's kings become more corrupt. The kingdom divides. The people fall into idolatry. The prophets begin to cry out for something greater—a kingdom not built by human hands, but one that would never end.

The need for God's Kingdom becomes undeniable.

The world was full of kings, but not one of them could fix what was broken. Not one of them could remove the power of sin and death.

Then, at a time when hope seemed lost, a star appears in the sky. Magi from the east—Gentiles—follow its light to a small town in Bethlehem, the city of David. And there, in a manger, lies the promised child.

"For there is born to you this day in the city of David a Savior, who is Christ the Lord" (Luke 2:11 NKJV).

A King has been born.

But He does not arrive in wealth or power. He is not born in a palace. He is laid in a feeding trough. His birth is not announced to rulers but to shepherds.

This is not the kingdom the people expected.

Jesus grows up, living a sinless life, resisting the very temptations that had overcome Adam and Eve. The serpent comes to Him in the wilderness, just as he had come to humanity in the garden, and offers Him an easier way. But Jesus refuses. *"It is written,"* He declares, holding firm to the truth of His Father.

Yet when He comes to His people, they do not recognize Him as King. They expected a Messiah who would overthrow Rome, not one who would suffer. They were looking for a lion, but John the Baptist pointed and said, *"Behold! The Lamb of God who takes away the sin of the world!" (John 1:29 NKJV).*

The people of Israel longed for the glory of David's throne to be restored. They expected their king to ride into Jerusalem on a warhorse, to raise an army, and to drive out their oppressors.

But instead, Jesus enters on a colt.

Why? Because His mission wasn't to wage war against Rome —it was to conquer death itself.

He was coming to Jerusalem not to take power, but to lay His life down. He was heading to Golgotha, to the cross. And the people, many of whom had just seen Him raise Lazarus from the dead, knew something was different about Him.

They followed, shouting *"Hosanna! Save us!"*

They were crying out for salvation, but they didn't yet realize what it truly meant.

This is why the Kingdom of God is needed. Not just for

Israel, but for the entire world. Every earthly kingdom had failed. Every human ruler had fallen short.

Sin still reigned. Death still ruled.

But the King had come.

And this time, He would not fail.

This is the story of the King and His Kingdom. This is the Gospel of Jesus Christ. It is not a fairy tale. It is not a story that begins with *"Once upon a time."* It is rooted in history. The Gospel is the fulfillment of every prophecy, every whisper, every longing throughout the Scriptures.

And now, through His death and resurrection, He invites us back into Eden—delight with God.

The same Jesus who entered Jerusalem as a Lamb will return again as a Lion. The King is coming again. This time, not on a colt, but on a white horse. This time, not to die, but to reign.

The serpent's head has been crushed. Death has lost its sting. The Kingdom of God is at hand.

And this... this is the good news that will bring great joy to all people.

Discussion Questions

1. The people of Jerusalem expected a political messiah to liberate them from Roman rule. How does Jesus' arrival on a colt, instead of a warhorse, challenge these expectations, and what does this contrast reveal about the nature of God's Kingdom as opposed to earthly kingdoms?

2. Reflecting on the Triumphal Entry and the subsequent events of Jesus' passion, how does the response of the crowd in Jerusalem ("Hosanna! Save us!") illustrate humanity's deep-seated recognition of its own brokenness and need for salvation? How does this scene enrich our understanding of salvation as more than just physical or political deliverance?

3. Discuss how the failures of earthly kingdoms and rulers throughout biblical history (from Egypt to Rome) underscore the necessity for the divine Kingdom of God. In what ways does the Kingdom of God, as exemplified by Jesus, provide a solution to the issues of sin and death that no earthly power could solve?

2

THE PROMISE OF THE KINGDOM

Everything that Jesus said was supposed to follow believers should follow believers—everything. I believe that Jesus' prayer, "Your kingdom come, Your will be done on earth as it is in heaven," should be and will be accomplished, and it's accomplished by the church.

When I talk to people and I ask, "What was the sum total of Jesus' message in the Gospels?" I get answers like, "Oh, it was love. If you were to get to the core of His message, it's about love." But that's not true. That's not the core of His message. In fact, in the synoptic Gospels, it is probably one of the smallest parts of His message. John, who wrote the last Gospel, writes about love. In the second half of the Gospel of John, he speaks more about love than all the other three Gospels combined because it wasn't the sum total of Jesus' message.

Other people will answer me, "The forgiveness of sin." They say, "If you're going to sum up Jesus' message, it's the forgiveness of sin." This also is not the focus or the sum of Jesus' ministry. The message and focus of the ministry of Jesus Christ is the Kingdom of God.

Jesus preached the Gospel of the Kingdom of God. That was the focus of His life and ministry. We will not understand the Gospels or the whole Bible if we don't understand the message of Jesus Christ. The sum and core of His message is the Kingdom of God.

"From that time Jesus began to preach and to say, "Repent, for the kingdom of heaven is at hand." Matthew 4:17 NKJV

The first thing you hear Jesus proclaim in Matthew chapter 4 is the Kingdom of God. John the Baptist? The same thing—the Kingdom of God. Jesus starts talking only half a chapter after John the Baptist. What's He proclaiming? The Kingdom of God. He went and preached about the Gospel of the Kingdom of God. As we will see, this was the focus of the life and ministry of Jesus Christ.

A large part of Jesus' teaching in the book of Matthew is found in chapters 5 through 7. It's what we call the "Sermon on the Mount". This is what we call the ethics of the Kingdom, or the ways of the Kingdom. We will focus on this in a later chapter. Then Jesus goes back to preaching the Gospel of the Kingdom. From chapter 8 on till the end of the Gospel of Matthew, why? Because that was the sum total of all His teachings—the Gospel of the Kingdom of God.

Jesus said, "If I cast out demons by the finger of God, you know the Kingdom of God has come upon you." Even the reason Jesus cast out demons was because of the Kingdom. Everything that Jesus talked about was centered on the Kingdom, and yet it's probably one of the most misunderstood topics today. Period. One of the reasons is that, for us in America, we're American. We don't even understand kingdoms. We're a democratic republic, so to us, we're like, "Kingdoms? Uh, is that like Great Britain?" In our modernized, Western world, we really don't understand kingdoms, which puts us at a disadvantage in our approach to the Gospel.

Kingdoms have to do with the rule and reign of a king. So, when Jesus proclaims a Kingdom is at hand and a Kingdom is coming, He is talking about the reign and rule of Someone. For us to understand this more completely, we have to go back to the Old Testament because, as I said before, if we read these Scriptures apart from understanding the message of the Kingdom, we will not see what Jesus wanted us to see in our lives—the manifestation of His Kingdom and will being done on earth as it is in heaven.

> *"And these signs will follow those who believe: In My name they will cast out demons; they will speak with new tongues; they will take up serpents; and if they drink anything deadly, it will by no means hurt them; they will lay hands on the sick, and they will recover."*
> *Mark 16:17-18 NKJV*

Probably all of us have been a part of, or seen, a church that talks a lot about the Scriptures, but the things Jesus said would follow believers don't follow believers. Then people will come to some churches where demons are being cast out in the lobby, and the leaders are not trying to hide it. The sick are being healed, and the people are just going after it. What's the difference? Understanding the Kingdom.

I went to Bible school, and you know how much they taught me about the Kingdom. Nothing. They never talked about it. I always joke and say I want my money back. The reason is, I tried ministry for ten years without understanding the message of the Kingdom, and you know how many people's lives I saw changed? How much healing and deliverance followed? Very little, at best. And it was really hard. I thought, "These people are sinners, and they won't stop sinning." I thought to myself, "I'm preaching repentance. I'm trying to get them to live free, and it's not happening. It's not working. How come?" Because I didn't understand the Gospel of the Kingdom, and the people didn't understand it either. So I said to myself, "I never want to do that again."

If Jesus' sole message was about the Kingdom of God, guess what the church's sole message is about? The Kingdom of God. We can see it in the book of Acts. In chapter 8, we read about Philip, the Evangelist.

"But when they believed Philip as he preached the things concerning the Kingdom of God and the name of Jesus Christ, both men and women were baptized." Acts 8:12 NKJV

The Scriptures also say he performed miracles, cast out unclean spirits, and healed many who were lame and paralyzed. So, there was great joy in that city. Then the apostles came down, and the believers were baptized in the Holy Spirit later in the chapter. So, guess what? This perfectly patterns what Jesus said would follow them—deliverance, healing, and they'd speak in new tongues. All of that happens in one little section in Acts, and it just happens over and over and over.

It happened in Jesus' life every single day, and it happened in the disciples' lives every single day. But it doesn't happen in most of our lives because we don't understand the Kingdom. But by the end of this book, I'm going to make sure we understand this whole thing by God's grace through the lens of Jesus Christ and the Kingdom of God.

Because of sin entering the world, there's now a need for a King to come. Adam and Eve had a King. They left His rule and reign, and they came under a new king who rules a kingdom of darkness. These are all themes in the Scriptures. The Bible talks about this age and the age to come. If you begin to understand this age and the age to come, you'll begin to understand Kingdom language. Jesus talked about the ruler of this age, and then the Lord, the new King of Kings. So, we have the ruler of this world or this age, and we have the King of the Kingdom of God, Jesus Christ—the King of the Kingdom that has come and is coming.

The whole Old Testament points to a King, a Kingdom, and to a new age. We see this over and over throughout the Scriptures. I want to show you, as quickly and concisely as possible, how you can catch this thread of the Kingdom of God throughout the Old Testament.

Something happened in the Old Testament. Adam and Eve sinned, this produced a need for the Kingdom of God. Sin enters the world, and when it does, death enters the world. Why? Because the wages of sin is death. So, death enters the world, and because one man sinned, all sinned. Because one man died, all die —until Jesus Christ. So, what we need to understand is that what was plaguing man at the beginning of the Bible, in Genesis chapter 3, is now still the same thing plaguing man today. It hasn't changed.

The reason that just wanting to be a good person doesn't work is because, in the very beginning, there was a perfect world where God's space and our space overlapped. It was awesome. Adam and Eve had no clothes on. If you're married and you don't have kids yet, you know what it was like—it's pre-kids, right? You're walking around the house in your birthday suit. No shame. And it's a wonderful world. God is walking freely through that place. It's a beautiful place. It's a Kingdom. God's rule is perfect.

But there was something in the Kingdom they weren't supposed to mess with. It was the tree of the knowledge of good and evil. They were never supposed to eat from it. There wasn't a point where it was like, "Well, okay, now we can eat from it." But

Adam and Eve made a decision that said they were better at determining what was good and evil than God was. God's like, "That tree is not for you. It'll lead to death. Don't eat it." So, Adam and Eve seemed to think, "Really? I don't know—maybe we're a better judge of what's good and not good, what's bad and not bad." So, this is how man turns away from the rule and reign of God.

Now, this is what we must understand: at any time in the Old Testament, do we ever see humans doing a good job at choosing and determining what's good and what's evil for themselves? No, we don't. Right away, Adam and Eve have children, and one kills the other.

Right away, he thinks this is good and right. How many of you have had children or been around children at some point? Are they good at determining right and wrong? None of us. Usually, we hear them say, "Mine!" and then they hit another kid. Did anyone have to teach them that? No. They go to someone else's house and still just say, "Mine." There's something inside of them from birth that is not good at judging what is right and what's wrong. They were born with a corrupted nature. So, we all must accept Jesus Christ to have the divine nature.

We see that from the time of Adam and Eve, there's this continual pattern of men determining what's right and what's wrong, what's good and what's evil, and they are not good at it. We see the flood with Noah because of this. We see the Tower of Babel because of this. They think it's a good idea to make a throne in the heavens for themselves, and God says, "That's not good. Let us confuse their language so that they can't continue to communicate with each other and do whatever evil is in their hearts to do." God's like, "We can't let that happen."

Again, in Genesis chapter 6, we see angels that sinned—the same thing. They decided to determine what's right and wrong for themselves instead of letting God determine that. They came and had relationships with women. They had children with them, and those children became the giants of the day. So, we see giants in the Promised Land, and they are these corrupt people, who have descended from this. This is all connected to the corruption in the hearts of men from Adam and Eve's choice to decide what's good and evil apart from God.

The Tower of Babel becomes an image throughout the rest of the Old Testament of this very problem. The problem is that when man gets power with a corrupted heart, they begin to corrupt. And when we see Egypt, Egypt becomes another example of this. Pharaoh becomes an image of Babel. He thinks, "You know what? These slaves are having too many kids. Let's kill their firstborn. Let's kill their boys—their male babies." This is not good, but he seems to think it is. In Pharaoh's mind, that was a good thing to do. Can you see how we are not good at judging?

And the same exact problem still exists today. Babel is still our problem today, and it is corrupting even the Church today. Today, people will say, "Well, I don't want this baby, so I'll just get rid of it." When we read about Pharaoh in the Bible, no one thinks, "This seems like a great guy." No, he's trying to kill babies and destroy families. And yet, in our society, we do it every day. And a lot of the Church has no problem with it. We say, "It's a woman's choice," which is the same as saying, "It's Pharaoh's choice." No, it's not your choice. Life is life. It belongs to the Lord, and you're not supposed to take it. It's sin.

The tree of the knowledge of good and evil is the same thing that corrupts Babel, corrupts Egypt, and enslaves God's people—His chosen people, Israel. So, Israel is now enslaved by this corrupted power, and God becomes a deliverer. This is the first time we see God as the God of salvation. He delivers His people from the hands of Pharaoh, which is like the hands of Babel, right? The corrupted hearts. Then the Lord leads Israel out of the waters in Exodus chapter 15, and they sing a song. They say these words:

"I will sing to the Lord, for He has triumphed gloriously! The horse and its rider He has thrown into the sea! The Lord is my strength and song, and He has become my salvation" Exodus 15:1-2 NKJV

This is the first time God is mentioned as the God of salvation. He's a rescuer, a deliverer. The word "salvation" means to rescue and to deliver. Israel then begins to call this event "The Day of the Lord". This language is so important—it's all through the Bible, even into the book of Revelation, "The Day of the Lord". This is directly connected to the message of the Kingdom. This will cause a lot of things in the Bible to stop appearing weird and to begin making sense.

Let's understand what "The Day of the Lord" is. It is when God shows up and makes things right. He brings judgment on those who have been unjust and delivers those who have been oppressed. It's "The Day of the Lord". This is what Israel celebrated and called "Passover". But they first called it "The Day of Yahweh", "The Day of the Lord". This becomes a central theme throughout the Scriptures, all the way through the Old Testament and even into the New Testament. The people of God are waiting on the Lord to bring about The Day of the Lord.

But as we read in the story, Israel goes into the Promised Land, and guess what happens? They become corrupted by Babel also. The wicked thing that says, "You're better at determining what's right and wrong, what's good and right, so you choose." So, they begin to choose, and we see this in the Scriptures, where kings begin to take land from people just because they want it. Queen Jezebel recognizes her husband's desire for something that's not his, it belongs to someone else and says, "I'll get it for you" (see 1 Kings 21). And they take the land from those it belongs to (Naboth and his family). Israel did many more things like this, and God's response through the prophets is essentially, "Okay, another day is coming, and when that day comes, it's like the court hearing has arrived, and the Judge will take His seat and He will make His verdict. Those who have been unjustly treated will be vindicated, and those who have unjustly treated people will be recompensed for their injustice."

The Day of the Lord is now coming, and all the prophets begin to talk about it—a day when Yahweh will have His justice. In Israel's mind, they think that it will be a good day. They're thinking, "There's a day coming, and it's going to be a good day." Then the prophets begin to say, "The wonderful Day of the Lord." And another prophet says, "The dreadful Day of the Lord." Israel is thinking, "Well, which one is it? Is it good or dreadful?" We must understand that our actions determine if it's a good or dreadful day. The Lord says in Micah:

"He has shown you, O man, what is good; and what does the Lord require of you but to do justly, to love mercy, and to walk humbly with your God?" Micah 6:8 NKJV

God says, don't worry about those who treat you unjustly and prosper. There will be a day of recompense and justice. They'll burn up like chaff. The Day of the Lord is coming. And guess what? The Day of the Lord does come—just not how they expected. Because part of God's message to Israel was that they had become the oppressors. They had become the very enemy God once delivered them from.

Babylon marches into Jerusalem and takes it. Now, Jerusalem is the city on a hill—the place where our light is supposed to shine from, a light like a city on a hill. Jerusalem is the city of peace. It's really hard to take a city on a hill. The one who's marching up to it has a disadvantage, especially if the city has a wall around it. Well, guess what? Jerusalem had a wall, and it was on top of a hill—very hard to take. So, Babylon comes in, and the prophets say, "They're coming." Jeremiah says, "Listen, this is not going to be good. The Lord's going to do this." And Israel says, "It's not possible," and in a moment, they're taken into captivity, and that is The Day of the Lord. Judgment was served, not on Israel's enemies—but on Israel, because they were the ones who were in transgression. They were stealing from the poor.

"Thus says the Lord: For three transgressions of Israel, and for four, I will not turn away its punishment, because they sell the righteous for silver, and the poor for a pair of sandals. They pant after the dust of the earth which is on the head of the poor, and pervert the way of the humble. A man and his father go in to the same girl to defile My holy name. They lie down by every altar on clothes taken in pledge and drink the wine of the condemned in the house of their god." Amos 2:6-8 NKJV

So, this is what's happening. A father and his son sleep with the same woman—the Bible says do not do that. Israel says, "But we want to." Their hearts have been corrupted by Babel. They are sleeping with temple prostitutes as an act of worship to a foreign god. Even though you're married, you sleep with the temple prostitute as an act of worship. One of the things happening here is found in the statement "clothes taken in pledge." Israel was taking the poor's clothes—it's their only garment, even their blanket at night. And the Scripture says:

"If you ever take your neighbor's garment as a pledge, you shall return it to him before the sun goes down. For that is his only covering; it is his garment for his skin. What will he sleep in? And it will be that when he cries to Me, I will hear, for I am gracious" Exodus 22:26-27 NKJV

So, Israel is taking the poor's clothes. Not only are they not returning them, but they are using them to sleep with the prostitutes on the steps of the temple. So, God says the Day of the Lord will come, and it does—Babylon comes and takes them into captivity.

Israel realized The Day of the Lord would be a day of judgment, but then there would be a day of salvation. So then, Israel begins to say, "Salvation has to come because we paid for this sin." And then Israel gets to go back home, and that's when Nehemiah and Ezra rebuild Jerusalem. But throughout this period of time, there begin to be whispers and murmurs of a coming King—a King like David, one who would sit on the throne of David.

Why David? Because David lived and reigned during the time of Israel's greatest success. David was a man after God's own heart, a virtuous man even with all his sins. So, David and his throne become this image of this coming King. God even prophesied to David, promising that someone from his lineage would sit on his throne forever. Israel began proclaiming that the King is coming and He will bring about The Day of the Lord—the salvation that they were supposed to get when they were released from Babylon because, when they came back, Jerusalem still lay in ruins. The promise in Isaiah 52 was that they would see Yahweh returning to Jerusalem and He would comfort His people. But that didn't happen when Israel was released from captivity.

Israel was whispering, "The Day of the Lord is coming," and Isaiah 40 talked about a wild man who would make straight the way in the wilderness and make ready the path of the coming of the Lord. Then John the Baptist comes on the scene, and he's preaching about the Kingdom of God. So now there is this merging between the Day of the Lord and the message of the Kingdom of God, and a message begins to arise about this age and the age to come.

This age is ruled by Satan, sin, death, and evil. It's the Babylon problem—the problem with the heart of man. It's this age that's ruled by Satan, but someone is going to come who is the seed of David, and He will bring an end to this age. It will be the Day of the Lord. John the Baptist said, "The winnowing fork is in His hand—the Day of the Lord is coming, the Kingdom of God is at hand." People began to ask, "What must we do?" John says, "Get baptized, wash away your sins, show that you're approved, and live rightly, because the Lord Yahweh is coming back to Jerusalem, so get ready." This is Israel's expectation: Yahweh is on His way—The Day of the Lord is going to come, and it's going to be a day of vengeance for the wicked. It's going to split time in half, and there will be that age and this age.

Then He comes, wrapped in cloth and laid in a manger not what they were expecting. In their minds, He was born in the wrong city. They had all these preconceived ideas of what the Messiah would be like. The evil of their day was Rome, so they thought He must be coming to take out Rome, and Israel would rule like David, and the Kingdom would be established physically again. So, the Day of the Lord comes in the person of Jesus Christ.

In a sense, the Day of the Lord is Calvary, and Jesus Himself takes on the real evil—not Rome. He lets sin, death, and evil take their best shot at Him. They lay all of their powers and weapons upon Him, and He takes them to the grave, and on the third day, He raises up. This also is a Day of the Lord. The cross was a day of judgment—your judgment and my judgment placed upon Him. And the resurrection is a day of salvation. It's a day when all who believe and call upon the name of the Lord, shall be delivered. It's a Day of the Lord. The day of judgment happens, and then the day of salvation happens. So, Jesus proclaims Isaiah 61:1-2:

"The Spirit of the Lord God is upon Me, because the Lord has anointed Me to preach good tidings to the poor; He has sent Me to heal the brokenhearted, to proclaim liberty to the captives, and the opening of the prison to those who are bound; to proclaim the acceptable year of the Lord." Isaiah 61:1-2 NKJV

He is proclaiming The Day of the Lord. It's also an image of Jubilee—the canceling of all debts. Israel never performed a Jubilee, and then Jesus Christ does the first one on the tree of Calvary, making it possible for all debts to be canceled and for everything (in this case us) to go back to its rightful owner (God).

So, you and I—we look back upon the Day of the Lord, and guess what the Scripture says? There is still another Day coming! And we, like John the Baptist, are supposed to proclaim the Gospel of the Kingdom, the coming of this King, the separation of this age and the age to come. They were expecting it to happen then, but our God is a gracious and merciful God, a long-suffering God—not wanting any to perish, but all to be saved.

So, there is a day coming—it's the white throne of judgment, and it's the Day of the Lord. Seals are being broken, and the Lamb of God is worthy to bring about another "Day". Revelation 21 talks about entering into the New Jerusalem. This is the Day of the Lord. The first day is the day of judgment before the white throne. Then the day of salvation—entering the New Jerusalem. Everything hinges around the Day of the Lord. Your salvation was made possible because of the Day of the Lord. And there is a day coming when there will no longer be an option for you, me, or anyone to repent. That day will come like a thief in the night. And if they are not ready, if they have not changed their garments, if they have not accepted the payment for their sins, when that day comes, there will be no more mercy.

So, the Church is God's herald, declaring the Day of the Lord is coming. Yahweh is coming. It will be a good day for those who put their trust in Jesus Christ. He is the only way in. His name literally means salvation. The only way into the city of salvation is through the person of salvation. He is the gate. He is the door. We must enter through Him.

Yeshuah—Yahweh is salvation. And for those who say, "All paths lead to God or to Heaven" no, they don't. The Bible says that Jesus said about Himself, "No one comes to the Father except through Me." He is the door to enter into eternity. So, the Day of the Lord, this age, and the age to come—the Kingdom of God—these things are all related. We are offering a dying, hurting, broken world the opportunity to be saved from drowning in their sin. But we must call upon the name of the Lord, and the rescue swimmer—Yahweh—will dive in to rescue us. But you must call upon His name, and you shall be delivered. You shall be saved from the powers of this world, and you'll become a new creation in Jesus Christ.

The fact that there is a day coming produces a zeal in us. Jesus says it will come upon us unexpectedly. So, if we still live according to the spirit of Babel and Babylon, it'll be a serious day. It is a serious thing for Yahweh to come upon you. It is a dreadful thing if you're not ready for the Lord.

This life is not to be played with. He says it's a vapor—here today, gone tomorrow. Be very careful with it. Be very careful. But for those who seek after righteousness and after His Kingdom, what does He say?

"Seek first the Kingdom of God and His righteousness, and all these things will be added to you." Matthew 6:33 NKJV

Seek that first. There's a stake that has been put in the ground at Calvary, and there's another stake. Only the Father knows when it will come. This is a period of grace and of the mercy of God. He is sitting like a swimmer, waiting for you to call out. But if you don't, you will not be saved, and it will not be His fault. He was there, ready, waiting for you to call.

Paul and Silas were in prison. For most of us, that would feel like drowning. But what did they do? They worshiped the Lord. They said, "This is the day the Lord has made. We should worship Him in it." They were excited. Guess what happened? The warden and his family began to be saved. Signs began accompanying these believers.

Now, you may be in a spiritual prison, and the powers of darkness and sin may still be drowning you. You may think, "I'm good. I believe in Jesus." But have you repented? Have you called upon the name of the Lord and truly, genuinely repented? Have you allowed Him to pull you out of that kingdom? You need to take those things of Babel and Babylon, get rid of them, and live a holy and righteous life in this age so that when the Day of the Lord comes, it will be a good day. It will be a celebrated day for you. Live in such a way that it will not be a fearful thing when that day comes, but a day of rejoicing. Amen.

Discussion Questions

1. How does recognizing the Kingdom of God as the central theme of Jesus' ministry influence your understanding of the Gospels?

2. In what practical ways can you prioritize seeking the Kingdom of God in your daily life?

3. Reflect on areas in your life where you might be relying on your own understanding of right and wrong instead of God's guidance. Why is it challenging for people to submit to God, and how can believers support each other in this journey?

4. What does the "Day of the Lord" signify for you personally, and how does it impact your outlook on life?

5. How can you actively live in readiness for this day and encourage others to do the same?

3

THE ARRIVAL OF THE KING

It is my desire that the Church would understand the entirety of the Scriptures, and I believe the best way to understand the Scriptures as a unified story—from Genesis to Revelation—is through the lens of the Kingdom of God. I see so many people who go to church, who love Jesus, and who read their Bible, but none of the things that Jesus said should follow believers are following them. I blame that on the Church. I don't blame that on the believers, so don't feel condemned. I just really want to see the Church be who God created her to be.

It was His intention that signs and wonders would follow the Gospel of the Kingdom as the evidence of salvation: healings, deliverance, and miracles (see Mark 16:17-18, Hebrews 2:4). The Kingdom should follow those who are citizens of the Kingdom everywhere they go. It followed Jesus, and it was His intent that it would follow our lives as well. But there are some things we have to realign in our hearts and minds for that to happen and one of those things is understanding the Kingdom of God.

As mentioned before, it's the sum total of Jesus' message. To understand more fully, we must first see that a King was promised, and now we must understand the arrival of the King. Why do we think Jesus' arrival had angels in heaven and on earth heralding "good news for all men", declaring a Savior is born? We say it at Christmas, but it is something we need to have in our hearts all the time because it's what the world needs—good news for all men.

When we open the Scriptures in Genesis, the word "Genesis" means "beginnings"—hence, "in the beginning". We see in the beginning that there is a good God who makes a good world, and He makes a garden. Then He places the only creation He created in His likeness in that garden to walk with Him and commune with Him. Other creatures were there, but they weren't made in His image and likeness. The image of God is placed upon these creatures that we call humans. They were put there to commune with God in this place where heaven and earth overlapped.

In our Western mindset, we have earth and then we have heaven, and in our minds, there is no connection between the two. But in the beginning, there was a complete connection between the two. There was an overlapping of God's space and our space. We walked in God's space, and God walked in our space.

We often think that one day we'll die and go to heaven if we believe in Jesus. As accurate as that is, it's not the central theme of the Scriptures. The theme of the Scriptures is that God is trying to bring heaven to earth. He's trying to fix the problem of "God's space" and "our space" being separated. To Him, the separation of our spaces is a problem. He wants our spaces to be one, for us to be one with Him in our space—His and ours included. That's why Jesus prayed and taught us to pray, "Your kingdom come, Your will be done on earth as it is in heaven." This is what He wants, and this is what He came for.

If we don't understand the entirety of the Scriptures with that purpose in mind, we'll miss the point. Heaven isn't about resting on clouds forever with little fat babies playing harps. That's not the picture of heaven, nor the picture of eternity. When people think that way, they think heaven looks boring because they're seeing a picture that someone else painted, not what the Scriptures teach.

Some think the Gospel is Jesus saying, "If you don't love Me, I'll send you to hell". That is not the Gospel—period. Sin leads to death. God so loved the world that He sent His Son to die on our behalf so we could receive His reward, which is life. This isn't about "love Me or I'll send you to hell". Our wrong choices sent us to hell, and God came and went to hell on our behalf so that we could dwell in His space and see heaven and earth reunited in a people.

This is the Gospel. We must see the Gospel clearly so that what we're sharing with others paints a clear picture of what God has communicated. God never intended to be separated from His children. The separation between God's space and our space happened because of humanity. Humanity chose to sit on a different throne than the one God gave them to rule with Him over creation. They sat on their own throne, ruling the way they wanted—deciding what was good and evil in their own eyes. Evil entered their hearts and brought the power of evil with it.

Scripture says that the serpent—who is called the devil and Satan, the dragon of old, the one that was in the garden—has filled their hearts and is now ruling over them as they sit on a throne with him, ruling the earth according to his ways. This leads to sin, death, and evil. Jesus says that Satan came to steal, kill, and destroy. That's what entered the hearts of humanity. Death was never God's plan or His intent for us. Eternal life was always the plan that The Father had for us. But when we chose sin, it led to death, just as He forewarned.

God even says to Cain, "Sin is knocking at your door. Don't open that door. It'll take your life." Cain opens the door, and it takes his brother's life and ultimately his own life. Sin leads to a city called Babel, where the same corruption that took hold of Cain corrupted the whole place. God says it's not good, and He divides the nations. But His plan was always to bring them back one day into one nation.

So, God picks a man named Abraham. He tells Abraham, "I'm going to make a nation out of you—a nation that blesses the earth instead of curses it." As we've discussed a hope arises that someone will come to redeem humanity. God says it will be Abraham's seed. Abraham has Isaac. Isaac has Jacob. Jacob has a son named Judah. Judah will hold the scepter, the symbol of a king. This one is going to be king. Moses sees this same king. He says, "A prophet greater than I."

"I will raise up for them a Prophet like you from among their brethren, and will put My words in His mouth, and He shall speak to them all that I command Him." Deuteronomy 18:18 NKJV

Balaam says, "A star shall come out of Jacob; a Scepter shall rise out of Israel." A star will be the sign of the King's arrival. Then we see in the Scriptures the picture of David's throne. God says to David:

"When your days are fulfilled and you rest with your fathers, I will set up your seed after you, who will come from your body, and I will establish his kingdom." 2 Samuel 7:12 NKJV

God is saying, someone is going to sit on your throne, David, and he's going to have a kingdom. So how come, in the New

Testament, Jesus' message is about a kingdom? Because it's about a King who has come to rule and reign. God said, "He will build a house for My name, and I will establish the throne of His kingdom forever." The story gets even better though. In verse 14, He says, "I will be His Father, and He will be My Son." Wait, what? Yahweh is going to be His Father? Not you, David. He will be your son, but ultimately I will be His Father, and He will be My Son.

So, now there's someone coming who is from Abraham, who is from Judah. What king was from Judah's line? King David. They thought, maybe it's David who is the promised king. It wasn't Saul—he wasn't from the line of Judah but from Benjamin. What's going on? David shows up, and they think, "Here's the king. He must be the one." He's the one holding the scepter. Well, it wasn't him, even though he was a man after God's own heart. He sinned too, gave way to the corruption of Babel, and died like the rest. So, there must still be someone to come who will sit on that throne, but when he comes, he'll be the Son of God.

Now, there's this mystery. I don't even think Satan understood. Satan is watching, listening to the prophets, and thinking, "I've got to kill this savior." We need to ponder this. We see these people whom Satan enters, like Pharaoh, and they kill all the firstborn. It's as if Satan knows a savior is coming—a deliverer who will rule as a king. It's like they understand the season and the hour. Satan understood the season and the hour of Moses' birth, so he began to kill all the babies. It's like they knew God was raising up a savior, and they had to stop it.

What happens in Jesus' day? Jesus has to escape to Egypt. Why? Herod gets word of a king, and he begins to kill all the children under two in the region where Jesus was born. Jesus has to flee to Egypt. It's like a replay of Egypt. The Scripture says, "Out of Egypt, I called My Son." That's what the Old Testament says. He's speaking about Israel in the Old Testament, but the New Testament writers use that to speak about Jesus. Because ultimately, we're talking about Jesus Christ.

Mankind had been waiting for this King, waiting for this King, waiting for this King. Israel believed that when they left Babylon, the promised King would come to deliver them and restore the kingdom. When they went to Babylon, that was the end of the kings. They named the kings all the way through Jesus' bloodline. They named the kings all the way through the line of David, through Solomon, and kept going. Then, when Israel was exiled to Babylon, the kings were all killed. Uh-oh. Israel comes out of Babylon, and they're thinking, 'who's going to be the king?'

Israel goes back to Jerusalem. The city of peace had been destroyed, but then we read in Isaiah 52 that when they would return to Jerusalem, a king would return. They would be singing. Good news! Good news! There would be these beautiful feet coming, announcing good news. What is the good news? The God of Israel lives. There's still a king in Israel, and he's returning. There's a king, and it's Yahweh! Therefore, when Israel leaves Babylon, they're waiting for that, and it doesn't happen. Now, they're back to waiting. Israel has their city back, but they are left without a king. They knew and believed a King would come and be from the line of Abraham, from Judah, from the throne of David. So, they waited. This is the expectation and frame of mind the first-century Jews and believers in Jesus were in.

When we open the New Testament, we see these words, and they don't make sense to Westerners in the 21st century, but they need to make sense. The very first words of Matthew, the first book in the New Testament are: "The book of the genealogy of Jesus Christ, the Son of David, the Son of Abraham." I'm telling you; the whole Bible is right there in that one verse. If you're Hebrew and you're living in that day, the Spirit of God would tell you that statement is true. You're doing the happy dance. You're like, "Are you kidding me?" We read it, and we're like, "Oh great, I've got to read the genealogy."

The word 'genealogy' in Greek is the word '*genesis*' and the name 'Jesus' means "Yahweh is salvation". Wait, what? This is the "Genesis of Yahweh is salvation, the son of David, the son of Abraham." Our hearts should be filled with joy. Are you telling me the King has come? Do you know what the word 'Christ' means? 'Christos'—the Messiah. 'Hamashiach' in Hebrew means 'Anointed One'. What did Samuel do to David? He anointed him, King.

So, Matthew 1:1 is saying this is "Yahweh is salvation, the Anointed One, the son of David, the son of Abraham." This is the One who would be a blessing to all nations, who would sit on a throne, and whose kingdom would never end. How can a man sit on a throne, and his reign never end? How can a man have a kingdom, and his kingdom never end? Because at some point, he'll die—oh, unless he conquers death. Unless He's the God-man. Satan didn't see it coming. Because if he had, he wouldn't have killed Jesus. He put his own nail in the coffin when he killed Jesus.

I want us to see Jesus because it will change everything. When we understand 'The Day of the Lord, and The Day of Yahweh', when He would come, and justice would be served on the wicked and the oppressed would be vindicated—who's going to do that? Yahweh. It's 'The Day of Yahweh', and then Yahweh shows up as a man.

Do you know what Yahweh means? 'I AM WHO I AM'. He is the Elohim of all Elohim. 'Elohim' means God or spiritual being. He is the only non-created spiritual being—the only spiritual being that was never created. He's like, Who am I? I AM that I AM. I AM whatever you need. That's who I am. I am the Solution to all your problems. I am your Deliverer. I am your Healer. I am the King of Israel. I am the King of the earth. I am the One who rides the clouds. I am the Ancient of Days. I am the Eternal One. This is who I am—Yahweh. That's His name, and He is all that and more to you and for you.

I want us to understand that they were looking for a king like David, and they got God. He just happened to be the descendant of Abraham, the descendant of David, and His name is Jesus—Yeshua. Yahweh is salvation is His name. This is the genesis, the beginning of Yahweh being Savior. He comes from David's throne. He's a descendant of Abraham. All of Israel would understand the implications of these words, and some people killed Jesus because of those words. In Matthew 1:18-21, it says:

> "Now the birth of Jesus Christ was as follows: After His mother Mary was betrothed to Joseph, before they came together, she was found with child of the Holy Spirit. Then Joseph her husband, being a just man, and not wanting to make her a public example, was minded to put her away secretly. But while he thought about these things, behold, an angel of the Lord appeared to him in a dream, saying, 'Joseph, son of David, do not be afraid to take to you Mary your wife, for that which is conceived in her is of the Holy Spirit. And she will bring forth a Son, and you shall call His name Jesus, for He will save His people from their sins.'" Matthew 1:18-21 NKJV

The word 'birth' is the word 'gennesis' in Greek. "The gennesis of Yahweh is salvation, the Anointed One." There's a whole sermon right there. You'll name Him 'God is salvation' because He will save His people from their sins. The word save is the word 'sozo', which means to save, heal, deliver, and make whole. Pause. Don't read over that. Who's He going to save? His people. What does He have to save them from? Not Rome—sin. So, He had to put on flesh in order to rescue and redeem His people in body, soul, and spirit because sin leads to death (Romans 6:23; James 1:13-15). He came to redeem His people and be their Savior.

We talked about this briefly in the last chapter. In Exodus 15, Yahweh becomes their Savior, and they begin to say that there's another day when Yahweh will be the Savior. Then He shows up in the flesh from the throne of David, and He's here to do what? Save His people from their sins. It goes on:

"So all this was done that it might be fulfilled which was spoken by the Lord through the prophet, saying: 'Behold, the virgin shall be with child, and bear a Son, and they shall call His name Immanuel,' which is translated, 'God with us.'" Matthew 1:22-23 NKJV

They didn't see it coming. They didn't see that it was going to be God Himself with us. They didn't see it. Satan didn't even see it, but now we can see it! I want you to see it too! In Matthew 2:13-17, it says:

"Now when they had departed, behold, an angel of the Lord appeared to Joseph in a dream, saying, 'Arise, take the young Child and His mother, flee to Egypt, and stay there until I bring you word; for Herod will seek the young Child to destroy Him.' When he arose, he took the young Child and His mother by night and departed for Egypt, and was there until the death of Herod, that it might be fulfilled which was spoken by the Lord through the prophet, saying, 'Out of Egypt I called My Son.' Then Herod, when he saw that he was deceived by the wise men, was exceedingly angry; and he sent forth and put to death all the male children who were in Bethlehem and in all its districts, from two years old and under, according to the time which he had determined from the wise men.

Then was fulfilled what was spoken by Jeremiah the prophet."
Matthew 2:13-17 NKJV

This is Joseph taking Jesus to Egypt because of Herod's intent to kill the newborn King, the Savior and Deliverer. In Matthew 3:1-3, it says:

"In those days John the Baptist came preaching in the wilderness of Judea, and saying, 'Repent, for the kingdom of heaven is at hand!' For this is he who was spoken of by the prophet Isaiah, saying: 'The voice of one crying in the wilderness: "Prepare the way of the Lord; Make His paths straight." Matthew 3:1-3 NKJV

This is powerful. God had been laying out His plan of salvation, and here, with the arrival of this promised King, John the Baptist declared, "Prepare the way of the coming of the Lord," not the coming of just a man. He used the word 'Lord'. Prepare for the coming of the Lord. He's quoting from Isaiah, and the original word is Yahweh. Prepare for the coming of God. Repent, for the kingdom of God is at hand, and I'm preparing the way of God's coming. God's on His way. It's the Day of the Lord. Then John sees a man and says, "Behold the Lamb of God, who takes away..." He has come and He has come to take away sin from the world. (John 1:29)

So, after all, it looks like Jesus didn't come to throw us into hell. No. Death came to do that. But He has come to take death and put it in the grave forever. This is what He's come to do: to defeat death and put it in the grave. And John the Baptist declares, This is the one, the blessed one.

Then, in verse 12, John says, "His winnowing fork is in His hand." This is imagery from Joel. The winnowing fork is in His hand. There will be a harvest at the end of time, and John says God has the winnowing fork in His hand for harvest. The harvest is here, and He will thoroughly clean His threshing floor and gather His wheat into His barn. He would gather His wheat into His barn and burn up the chaff—the stuff that doesn't belong on the wheat, which represents us. It's the sin and the evil. He would put it through fire, thus causing this separation.

In Matthew 3, Jesus goes to John the Baptist and says, "I need to be baptized." John's like, "No, I'm not worthy to even tie your sandals. I'm not baptizing You. You need to baptize me. I know You have an awesome baptism—I want it right now!" But Jesus says, "No, you need to baptize me so that it can be fulfilled." So, John the Baptist baptizes Him. In verse 16-17, it says:

"When He was baptized, Jesus came up immediately from the water, and behold, the heavens were opened to Him, and the Spirit of God descended like a dove and alighted upon Him. And suddenly a voice came from heaven, saying, 'This is My beloved Son, in whom I am well pleased.'" Matthew 3:16-17 NKJV

If we are catching this, we'll see that this is fulfilling God calling the Son of David His Son. Yahweh calls 'Yahweh is Salvation' His Son. David would have someone who would be on his throne, and He would be a King who would sit on a throne and His kingdom would never end—and He would be God's Son.

John the Baptist is saying this is the one who will take away the sins of the world. This is the blessed one the Scriptures talked about. Then heaven declares in affirmation, This is the One. The Spirit of God bears witness, This is the One. The heavens are torn open. In the Old Testament, the heavens would be torn open in Isaiah 64:1, which says that He would pour out His Spirit. Here in Matthew 3, we see the fulfillment, and the anointing falls upon the Son of David—the Anointed One.

In the next chapter of Matthew, Jesus goes into the wilderness like Israel did after coming out of Egypt. The seas were parted for Israel at the Red Sea, and they went into the wilderness. Jesus goes into the waters of baptism, the waters are parted, and then He goes into the wilderness. Satan comes to tempt Him, just as Israel was tested in the wilderness, and says, "If You are the Son, then turn this rock into bread and eat." He's here to question whether or not Jesus is the Son of God.

We have this man—He's the Son of David, the Son of Abraham—but here's the twist: He's the Son of God. But what did Jesus call Himself? Jesus knows He's the Son of God, but He calls Himself the 'Son of Man'. Where does this term come from? The book of Daniel. Daniel was one of the most amazing prophets—this guy saw to the end. God let Daniel see the end. Most of John's revelation is seeing what Daniel got to see before him. Daniel gets to see this amazing thing.

Daniel's vision begins in Daniel chapter 2, where King Nebuchadnezzar has a dream and wants someone to interpret it. Daniel is the only one able to do it. Daniel tells him the dream: there was a stone cut out without human hands, and it struck this statue. The statue represented different kingdoms. The stone struck the feet of iron and clay and broke them into pieces. The iron, the clay, the bronze, the silver, and the gold were all crushed together and became like chaff.

Remember what John the Baptist said? "There's going to be a harvest, and the chaff is going to be blown away." Daniel saw this hundreds of years before. He said, "The iron, clay, bronze, silver, and gold were crushed together and became like chaff from the summer threshing floors; the wind carried them away so that no trace of them was found." Those represent the kingdoms of the earth. The kingdoms of the earth collapse. God blows them away, and they were never seen again. John the Baptist says they're thrown into the fire. Then Daniel says the stone that struck the image became a mountain, and it filled the whole earth. Jesus is that stone. They were waiting for a stone to come and strike the nations, causing the nations to fall, for His Kingdom to arise and fill the earth.

So, when we open Matthew, it's like the King has come. David's descendant, who will be King and whose Kingdom will never end, has arrived. He's the descendant of Abraham and David, but even more, He's the descendant of Yahweh. He's God's Son, and His Kingdom will last forever and fill the earth. They were waiting for it. We have received it. The Scripture says they all waited for the promise, but we've received the promise. Later, in Daniel 7:13, we read:

"I was watching in the night visions, And behold, One like the Son of Man, Coming with the clouds of heaven!" Daniel 7:13 NKJV

What a boss. One like the Son of Man—He's a man, but He's riding the clouds! I hope we're catching what's happening, Church. He's a man, yet He can ride the clouds. The Scripture continues:

"He came to the Ancient of Days, And they brought Him near before Him." Daniel 7:13 NKJV

The Son of Man hopped on a cloud and rode it to the Ancient of Days. Jesus says to His disciples, "I go to prepare a place for you," and He spends forty days after the resurrection telling them about the Kingdom of God. Then He takes off on a cloud to the Ancient of Days to take His throne. Daniel continues:

"Then to Him was given dominion and glory and a kingdom, that all peoples, nations, and languages should serve Him. His dominion is an everlasting dominion, which shall not pass away,

And His kingdom the one which shall not be destroyed." Daniel 7:14 NKJV

They were waiting for a King. What a King we've received!

"I was watching; and the same horn was making war against the saints and prevailing against them, until the Ancient of Days came, and a judgment was made in favor of the saints of the Most High, and the time came for the saints to possess the kingdom." Daniel 7:21-22 NKJV

Who are the saints? The believers—the ones the Son of Man made into saints by His blood. The horn? This is imagery of a nation that comes against the saints. They were waiting for a Kingdom. This is the entirety of the Scriptures. Satan had become a king in a sense over the people of God, but God would send a new King from Abraham who would make it possible for His saints, His holy ones, to enter His Kingdom forever. This is their hope. Then Jesus shows up as that hope.

Jesus says in Mark 14:61, as He is being interrogated before they kill Him, the Jewish priests are questioning God, wondering who He is because they missed Him. Because religion misses it every time. The high priest asks Him, "Are you the Anointed One? Are you the Messiah, the Son of the Blessed?" They wouldn't say Yahweh's name—they called Him 'the Blessed'. Jesus responds, "I AM." It's like when Moses asked, "Who should I say sent me?" and God said, "Tell them I AM sent you."

The high priest asked, "Are you the Son of the Blessed?" Jesus responds, "I AM." If you're looking for someone to redeem Israel, look no further. I AM has arrived. He continues, "I am. And you will see the Son of Man sitting at the right hand of the Power, and coming with the clouds of heaven" (Mark 14:62 NKJV). 'When you see Me again, you'll say, 'Blessed', because I'll be riding the clouds. If you miss Me now, you'll catch Me then. You will have no question whether it's Me—I'll be riding clouds to the Ancient of Days, making a way for the saints to come into the Kingdom of God forever.'

He is going to make the nations rage against the saints. But He says the Ancient of Days will come and make a judgment in favor of the saints, and they will come into the Kingdom. So, give thanks! He's delivered us from the power of the kingdom of darkness and brought us into the Kingdom of His Son of His love. This is Jesus who will save His people from their sins. Who are His people? The saints—those who believe in Him and receive redemption by His blood.

I want us to see Jesus. May we not miss Him. Let the full Gospel and the truth of these words penetrate your heart. Your life will be like no ordinary life. Signs, wonders, and miracles will be normal. They follow those who believe. As John the Baptist said, let us behold, let us love the Lord, and see who He is in all His fullness according to the Scriptures.

Now, I'm going to go through fifty titles given to the Son of Man—all because He is everything you need.

- He is the Almighty (Revelation 1:8).
- He is all authority (Matthew 28:18).
- He is the image of the invisible God (Colossians 1:15).
- He is the Alpha and Omega (Revelation 1:8).
- He is the First and the Last (Revelation 22:13).
- He is our advocate with the Father (1 John 2:1).
- He is the Bread of Life (John 6:35).
- He is our wellspring of life (John 6:35).
- He is the Beloved (Matthew 3:17).
- He is the Bridegroom (Matthew 9:15).
- He is the Chief Cornerstone (Psalm 118:22).

- He is the Deliverer from wrath to come (1 Thess 1:10).
- He is Faithful and True (Revelation 19:11).
- He is the Good Shepherd (John 10:11).
- He is the High Priest (Hebrews 3:14).
- He is the Head of the Church (Ephesians 1:22).
- He is the Holy Servant (Acts 4:29).
- He is the I AM (John 8:58).
- He is the Gift (2 Corinthians 9:15).
- He is the Judge (Acts 10:41).
- He is the King of Kings (Revelation 17:14).
- He is the Lamb of God (John 1:29).
- He is the Light of the World (John 8:12).
- He is the Lion of the Tribe of Judah (Revelation 5:5).
- He is Lord of All (Philippians 2:9-11).
- He is our Mediator (1 Timothy 2:5).
- He is the Messiah (John 1:41).
- He is the Mighty One of Jacob (Isaiah 60:16).
- He is the One who sets us free (John 8:36).
- He is our Hope (1 Timothy 1:1).
- He is our Peace (Ephesians 2:14).
- He is our Prophet (Mark 6:4).
- He is our Redeemer (Job 19:25).
- He is the Risen Lord (1 Corinthians 15:3-4).
- He is our Rock (1 Corinthians 10:4).
- He is the Atoning Sacrifice (1 John 4:10).
- He is our Savior (Luke 2:11).
- He is the Son of Man (Luke 19:10).
- He is the Son of the Most High (Luke 1:32).
- He is the Supreme Creator (Colossians 1:16-17).
- He is the Resurrection and the Life (John 11:25).
- He is the Door (John 10:9).
- He is the Way, the Truth, and the Life (John 14:6).
- He is the Word (John 1:1).
- He is the Vine (John 15:1).
- He is the Truth (John 8:32).

- He is the Victor (Revelation 3:21).
- He is the Wonderful Counselor (Isaiah 9:6).
- He is the Everlasting Father (Isaiah 9:6).
- He is the Prince of Peace (Isaiah 9:6).

Colossians 1:12-20 (NKJV) says, "Giving thanks to the Father who has qualified us to be partakers of the inheritance of the saints in the light. He has delivered us from the power of darkness and conveyed us into the kingdom of the Son of His love, in whom we have redemption through His blood, the forgiveness of sins. He is the image of the invisible God, the firstborn over all creation. For by Him all things were created that are in heaven and that are on earth, visible and invisible, whether thrones or dominions or principalities or powers. All things were created through Him and for Him. And He is before all things, and in Him all things consist. And He is the head of the body, the church, who is the beginning, the firstborn from the dead, that in all things He may have the preeminence. For it pleased the Father that in Him all the fullness should dwell, and by Him to reconcile all things to Himself, by Him, whether things on earth or things in heaven, having made peace through the blood of His cross."

He is the I AM. He is the Son of Man. This is Jesus Christ, the Son of David, the Son of Abraham. There's a King in heaven who has brought about a Kingdom, and He's inviting you to be a part of the Kingdom of Heaven. This King wants to be all that you need.

Are you thirsty? He's the wellspring. Are you hungry? He's the Bread of Life. Do you need healing? He's the Healer. Do you need redemption? He's the Redeemer. His name is Jesus, the Son of Man, the Son of God, our Savior. Receive Jesus Christ as the I AM of your life.

Discussion Questions

1. How does viewing the entire Bible through the lens of the Kingdom of God influence your understanding of Scripture and your daily walk of faith? In what practical ways can the church today realign its focus to emphasize the Kingdom of God and experience the signs and wonders the scriptures testify of?

2. How do the Old Testament prophecies about a coming King enhance your appreciation of Jesus' mission and identity? What impact does acknowledging Jesus as both the descendant of David and the Son of God have on your personal faith journey?

3. What does it mean to you that God's plan involves bringing heaven to earth rather than just bringing people to heaven? How can this understanding shape the way you live out your faith and share the Gospel with others?

4

THE WAY OF THE KINGDOM

When the King showed up, He had a way of doing business; I call this the way of the Kingdom. We're going to understand why Jesus did what He did, why He said that we should do the same, and how we can do that. Let's look at the very beginning of Jesus' ministry and the first words that we find Jesus preaching.

> *"From that time Jesus began to preach and to say, 'Repent, for the kingdom of heaven is at hand.'" Matthew 4:17 NKJV*

The message He had was: there's a Kingdom. Heaven has a Kingdom, and it's coming to earth—it's at hand, it's here. John the Baptist said the same words: repent, basically turn away from the kingdom of darkness and the rule of evil, and get ready, for the Kingdom of light is at hand. Then John sees Jesus and says, "The Lamb of God who will save the world from their sins. The One who's going to save us from the kingdom of darkness is here! I saw the Spirit of God descend upon Him like a dove." Jesus gets baptized, the heavens open, and He is anointed with power as the King to bring the Kingdom. No longer, in a sense, is the Kingdom just at hand—it is here in the person of Jesus Christ. The Kingdom came in the person of the King.

People will say it's all in the future. Well, the King already showed up, and He knighted some people and then said, "I'm coming back." When He came, it was like the inauguration of the Kingdom, and now there's a consummation coming. I'm excited for the consummation of the Kingdom. But let us not forget—it's already been inaugurated, and it was inaugurated by Jesus Christ. We are in between the inauguration and the consummation—it's already a Kingdom. Jesus is here saying, "The Kingdom has arrived." The rule and reign of God on earth have begun in the person of Jesus Christ. Then He asks some fishermen to follow Him, be His disciples, be His students. He's going to equip them and prepare them for the work of the Kingdom.

> *"And Jesus went about all Galilee, teaching in their synagogues, preaching the gospel of the kingdom." Matthew 4:23 NKJV*

What was Jesus teaching? What gospel did Jesus have? A Kingdom gospel—not a gospel of salvation alone. That's a part of the gospel of the Kingdom. I'm not saying it's not the gospel; it's just part of it. Paul talked about the full gospel. I wonder why he had to, in his own lifetime, use the term "full gospel"—because people were already starting to lean on the partial gospel. Look at what Paul said in Romans:

> *"In mighty signs and wonders, by the power of the Spirit of God... I have fully preached the gospel of Christ." Romans 15:19 NKJV*

This clearly reveals that without the power of the Spirit of God, we will only partially preach the gospel, which is an injustice to the Lord Jesus Christ. The gospel can be witnessed with the finger of God, the power of God. So we declare that the Kingdom has come, and then we can show that it's come by a demonstration of the Spirit and power. Christ was, and we are, making this space like Heaven's space by removing things that don't belong in God's space.

> *"And healing all kinds of sickness and all kinds of disease among the people. Then His fame went throughout all Syria; and they brought to Him all sick people who were afflicted with various diseases and torments, and those who were demon-possessed, epileptics, and paralytics; and He healed them. Great multitudes followed Him." Matthew 4:23-25 NKJV*

The testimony of the Kingdom witnessed with power caused Jesus' fame to spread throughout the region so that they brought to Him all the sick people afflicted by various diseases and torments and those who were demon-possessed, epileptics, or paralytics and He healed them. Why? Because none of those things are in His Father's Kingdom. Then He goes into the Sermon on the Mount. He has disciples now. He climbs up a mountain or a hill, His disciples follow Him, and some masses of people as well. And He gives them what I would call the ethics of the Kingdom. That's what the Kingdom's culture is like.

There's a way of the Kingdom—it has power and ethics. They're both a part of it. We need the ethics, we need the character of the Kingdom, and we need the power as well. Our internal world should match the external world of the Kingdom. If they don't, watch for failures—when someone moves in a greater anointing than they do character, usually there will be failure.

Ethics are not the focus of this chapter—we'll dive into that in the next chapter. I want to focus on the way of the Kingdom. Matthew chapters 5 through 7 are all about the ethics. In chapter 8, Jesus comes back down and goes back into modeling the way of the Kingdom. This is Him walking around, just doing life. Jesus is just being an Anointed One, going from town to town, just being a child of God, like you and I were created to be. What does it look like when Jesus goes on a stroll? People get saved, healed, and delivered. That's what it looks like. He just goes on a daily walk, and people get saved, healed, and delivered. Guess what it should look like when you go for a walk? People should get saved, healed, and delivered. Think about it. The Scripture says:

"When He had come down from the mountain, great multitudes followed Him. And behold, a leper came and worshiped Him, saying, 'Lord, if You are willing, You can make me clean.' Then Jesus put out His hand and touched him, saying, 'I am willing; be cleansed.' Immediately his leprosy was cleansed." Matthew 8:1-3 NKJV

What does the Kingdom look like? Leprosy disappearing—that's what it looks like. But wait, there's more:

"Now when Jesus had entered Capernaum, a centurion came to Him, pleading with Him, saying, 'Lord, my servant is lying at home paralyzed, dreadfully tormented.' And Jesus said to him, 'I will come and heal him.' The centurion answered and said, 'Lord, I am not worthy that You should come under my roof. But only speak a word, and my servant will be healed. For I also am a man under authority, having soldiers under me. And I say to this one, "Go," and he goes; and to another, "Come," and he comes; and to my servant, "Do this," and he does it.' When Jesus heard it, He marveled, and said to those who followed, 'Assuredly, I say to you, I have not found such great faith, not even in Israel! And I say to you that many will come from east and west, and sit down with Abraham, Isaac, and Jacob in the kingdom of heaven. But the sons of the kingdom will be cast out into outer darkness. There will be weeping and gnashing of teeth.' Then Jesus said to the centurion, 'Go your way; and as you have believed, so let it be done for you.' And his servant was healed that same hour." Matthew 8:5-13 NKJV

This speaks to those who don't come in by faith but by the works of the law—they'll be cast out, and those they didn't expect to come in, like Gentiles, will come right in by faith. Right away, we see leprosy disappear, and a person a long distance away is healed—two healings. Then, at Peter's mother-in-law's house, she is sick with a fever. Jesus touches her hand, and the fever leaves her. She gets up and serves them—*Bang*—three healings, and we're not even halfway through the chapter.

Then that evening, they brought to Him those who were demon-possessed, and He cast out the spirits with a word. He healed all who were sick, that it might be fulfilled which was spoken by Isaiah the prophet: "He Himself took our infirmities and bore our sicknesses." It just never seems to end in the gospels, and that's what it's going to look like every day. It continues with the believers in the book of Acts after Jesus ascends back to Heaven. There's a character to the Kingdom, the way we treat each other and the way we relate to God. But then, there's also a way of the Kingdom, which is when we carry what the world needs.

My question is: Why did Jesus' ministry look this way? We need to understand why Jesus' ministry looked this way so we can learn from Him and model it in ourlives. Why was there the healing of the sick and the casting out of demons seemingly every single time He went for a walk or even when He was trying to get away? Jesus might have needed a retreat, yet people flocked to Him. And instead of meeting His own needs, He feeds them and continues His ministry. Why does He keep doing this? Why does He keep performing miracles, signs, and wonders?

How come so many people are on one side saying, "Oh, it's just about salvation and waiting to go to Heaven. Then the good stuff will happen"? That side would say Jesus was doing miracles solely because He was God, proving He was God. Therefore, believers have no responsibility to do them because, well, we're not God, right?

But, that doesn't explain why Jesus said that we should do the same things. He said, "Everything I did and taught you, that's what you're going to do and teach others." So then, this becomes awkward—are we supposed to do this stuff or not? To say that we aren't, because that would be us acting like God, is to ignore Jesus' command. And to not do it is to disobey what Jesus commanded us to do. So, many of us just sit and wait, unsure if we're right or wrong.

That's a dangerous mindset, and it's why it will be a troubling day for many believers. That's what burns inside of me—because it doesn't have to be. This thing is simple. It's not complicated. This is really, really simple. But so many trusted teachers have taught things that are so contrary to Scripture, but they were trusted. So, people say, "Well, my pastor told me..." And then I say, "But what does the Bible say?" Your pastor might be a nice guy, but someone lied to him, who was lied to by someone else, and behind it all is Satan—it's the doctrines of demons.

When you read about the doctrines of demons in 1 Timothy and 2 Timothy, and then you look at the camp of Christians who say miracles are not for today, it's like, 'Oh my gosh!' It literally says they search the Scriptures, but deny the power that could save them, having a form of godliness but denying its power. And what's the main thing they deny? The power. They're like, "The power is not needed today because that was only for the apostles to prove they were apostles and that their words were the Scriptures."

That belief system cannot truly understand any of the Scriptures. It's like the blind leading the blind. There's nothing in the New Testament that you can understand with that mindset. You won't understand Jesus. You won't understand His Kingdom. You won't understand yourself or the Church. You won't understand what is promised. They use the Scriptures to deny what the scriptures promise. It doesn't make any sense.

I want you to forget what anyone else said and read the Bible for yourself, like 30 times, and at the end of it, tell me if you can possibly believe what cessationists tell you. There are way too many Scriptures you have to throw out to believe that. Don't do that—especially the commands of Jesus. Some will be in big trouble when they stand before Jesus. This is one reason I want to really see us get grounded in the Old Testament and New Testament as one story about the Kingdom of God. It's all the same story. Maybe that's why they don't understand the New Testament—because they don't understand the Old Testament, the Day of the Lord, the Kingdom of God, the Anointed One.

Let's look at Isaiah chapter 60. This is a cornerstone to understanding the Kingdom of God. There are many more Scriptures we could go through, but this is one to remember:

> *"Arise, shine; For your light has come! And the glory of the Lord is risen upon you. For behold, the darkness shall cover the earth, And deep darkness the people; But the Lord will arise over you, And His glory will be seen upon you. The Gentiles shall come to your light, And kings to the brightness of your rising." Isaiah 60:1-3 NKJV*

It's speaking about Jesus. Let's continue in verse 16. Open your Bible and read the whole thing on your own—it's all so good. Verses 11 through 12 are awesome. The second half of the chapter talks about the favor, the riches, and all that's going to come with the Kingdom:

> *"You shall know that I, the Lord, am your Savior and your Redeemer, the Mighty One of Jacob." Isaiah 60:16 NKJV*

What's Jesus' name? "Savior." He says, "You will know that the Lord," the word there is Yahweh, "You will know that Yahweh is your Savior." Then Jesus shows up, and His name is Yeshua, which means Yahweh is Salvation. I wonder who this is talking about—your Redeemer, the Mighty One of Jacob. It's Jesus! Verse 18 gives a little imagery there in the second half of it:

"I will also make your officers peace, And your magistrates righteousness. Violence shall no longer be heard in your land, Neither wasting nor destruction within your borders; But you shall call your walls Salvation, And your gates Praise." Isaiah 60:17-18 NKJV

This is very important— "Your walls will be called Salvation." This points us to another related Scripture:

"The sun shall no longer be your light by day, Nor for brightness shall the moon give light to you; But the Lord will be to you an everlasting light, And your God your glory. Your sun shall no longer go down, Nor shall your moon withdraw itself; For the Lord will be your everlasting light, And the days of your mourning shall be ended. Also your people shall all be righteous; They shall inherit the land forever, The branch of My planting, The work of My hands, That I may be glorified." Isaiah 60:19-21 NKJV

The Lord says, "I'm going to plant them. They're going to be the work of My hands. They're going to bear fruit, and it's going to give Me glory."

Then we come to Isaiah 61, which is key to understanding the New Testament. If we don't study this and understand the New Testament based on this person in Isaiah 61, we won't understand Jesus. Hundreds and hundreds of years before Jesus, the Scriptures were talking about Him over and over and over. Don't miss Him.

If we don't see what the Scriptures, the Old Testament Scriptures, say about Jesus, we'll miss it. Remember, the early believers in the 1st century only had the Old Testament before the New Testament was written. When we read the New Testament, the early Church only had the Old Testament, and they began to receive letters from the apostles. But it wasn't considered, in a sense, a New Testament yet. You can find all of the New Testament witnessing about Jesus in the Old Testament. Isaiah 61 is a prime example:

"The Spirit of the Lord God is upon Me, Because the Lord has anointed Me To preach good tidings to the poor; He has sent Me to heal the brokenhearted, To proclaim liberty to the captives, And the opening of the prison to those who are bound; To proclaim the acceptable year of the Lord, And the day of vengeance of our God; To comfort all who mourn, To console those who mourn in Zion, To give them beauty for ashes, The oil of joy for mourning, The garment of praise for the spirit of heaviness; That they may be called trees of righteousness, The planting of the Lord, that He may be glorified."
Isaiah 61:1-3 NKJV

You see it again—He's going to plant something, and it's going to be you. You're going to be oaks of righteousness, and you're going to bring glory to the Lord. We're going to see that in the New Testament as well.

"And they shall rebuild the old ruins, They shall raise up the former desolations, And they shall repair the ruined cities, The desolations of many generations. Strangers shall stand and feed your flocks, And the sons of the foreigner shall be your plowmen and your vinedressers. But you shall be named the priests of the Lord, They shall call you the servants of our God. You shall eat the riches of the Gentiles, And in their glory you shall boast. Instead of your shame you shall have double honor, And instead of confusion they shall

rejoice in their portion. Therefore in their land they shall possess double; Everlasting joy shall be theirs." Isaiah 61:4-7 NKJV

It's just amazing. It's all beautiful—everlasting joy, the great joy of the Lord. Reading it through the lens of a King and a Kingdom is what makes it so beautiful. Otherwise, it's like, 'What are they talking about? What's going on?'. When we understand Jesus and then read the Old Testament, it's like, 'He's everywhere! This whole thing is about Jesus!'

Let's check out Luke chapter 4. This is Luke's account paralleling Matthew's account of how Jesus started His ministry. It gives us something Matthew left out that happened between Matthew chapters 3 and 4, but Luke records it. This is Luke's purpose—when you read the beginning of Luke, he's like, "Hey, Theophilus, many people have ventured out to give an account of Jesus. I want to give a full collection of what I've heard from the different apostles."

"So He came to Nazareth, where He had been brought up. And as His custom was, He went into the synagogue on the Sabbath day, and stood up to read. And He was handed the book of the prophet Isaiah. And when He had opened the book, He found the place where it was written: 'The Spirit of the Lord is upon Me, Because He has anointed Me To preach the gospel to the poor; He has sent Me to heal the brokenhearted, To proclaim liberty to the captives And recovery of sight to the blind, To set at liberty those who are oppressed; To proclaim the acceptable year of the Lord.' Then He closed the book, gave it back to the attendant, and sat down. And the eyes of all who were in the synagogue were fixed on Him. And He began to say to them, 'Today this Scripture is fulfilled in your hearing.' So, all bore witness to Him and marveled at the gracious words which proceeded out of His mouth." Luke 4:16-22 NKJV

This story ends with them wanting to kill Him. Why?

Because He just said He's the Anointed One. He's the 'hamashiach', the word for Christ. He is the Christ, the Savior, the Messiah. He's the Deliverer of Israel. That's what He just claimed, and they're like, "No, you're not! You're from here—we know your mom, and your siblings!" And so, they try to kill Him. But it doesn't work. Jesus died when He wanted to die, not before.

Jesus believed He was the Anointed One and Isaiah 60 says when the Anointed One comes, He's going to do something. Isaiah says, "The sun will be no more, salvation will be your walls." If we've read the end of the book, that's Revelation 21.

"Now I saw a new heaven and a new earth, for the first heaven and the first earth had passed away. Also there was no more sea. Then I, John, saw the holy city, New Jerusalem, coming down out of heaven from God, prepared as a bride adorned for her husband. And I heard a loud voice from heaven saying, 'Behold, the tabernacle of God is with men, and He will dwell with them, and they shall be His people. God Himself will be with them and be their God.'"
Revelation 21:1-3 NKJV

Well, who is Jesus? 'Emmanuel, God with us.' John says, "I saw God with them." God will wipe away every tear from their eyes; there shall be no more death, nor sorrow, nor crying. There shall be no more pain, for the former things have passed away. Then in verse 22:

"But I saw no temple in it, for the Lord God Almighty and the Lamb are its temple. The city has no need of the sun or the moon to shine in it, for the glory of the Lord illuminates it. The Lamb is its light." Revelation 21:22-23 NKJV

John says he sees walls come down when he sees the New Jerusalem coming down, and Isaiah said, "You shall call your walls Salvation, and your gates Praise. You don't need the sun or the moon." He was talking about the Kingdom of God. He's talking about the fullness of the Kingdom of God—no more pain, no more suffering. None. All of that's gone forever.

So Jesus is bringing that about. This is what we have to understand: the reason why Jesus went about healing the sick is because there's no sickness in the Kingdom. Revelation 21 is the fullness of the Kingdom, and there are no sick people there. None. Zero sick people in the fullness of the Kingdom. Why? Because in Revelation 20, at the White Throne of Judgment, Satan has been thrown with all of his workers into the lake of fire forever. So, who's causing sickness on earth? Satan.

"how God anointed Jesus of Nazareth with the Holy Spirit and with power, who went about doing good and healing all who were oppressed by the devil, for God was with Him." Acts 10:38 NKJV

So when we understand sickness—COVID, whatever it is—it's the devil. When we succumb to sickness, we're under attack from the devil. When the devil leaves, sickness leaves. All forms of it. So how can a church not do deliverance? How come the Church is as sick as the world is? We just leave out one of the biggest ministries that Jesus did—He went about healing the sick and casting out demons.

Of course, we know not all sickness is a demon. If I get hit by a car and break my leg, and I need healing, that wasn't a demon. I broke my leg from a car accident, and I need healing. I need what's going to happen naturally to happen, right? As a child of God, my leg would heal—maybe not right away, but it would heal. It would naturally happen. Jesus just says, "Let it be done now. Let the future come now." That's what He's doing—He's bringing what's in the fullness of the Kingdom here now.

When Jesus raises the dead, it's because there are no dead

people in Revelation 21—the resurrection has happened. Even death, Hades, and the sea give up their dead in Revelation 20. And they're judged. Everyone is judged according to their works. You will be judged by your works. You're not saved by your works, but you are judged by them. So, it's about faith—that's how we enter the Kingdom. We don't get into the Kingdom by works. Our works will never get us into the Kingdom. Only faith gets you into the Kingdom.

At the end of your life, you will be judged by your work. Once you've entered the Kingdom, He gives us work to do, and we'll be judged by it. So, this group that doesn't believe in the power of the Holy Spirit is for today says, "Let's just sit down and wait." Don't do it—you're going to be judged by your works. They'll get into the Kingdom. The Scripture says many of them will get in, but they'll get in naked.

"For we are God's fellow workers; you are God's field, you are God's building. According to the grace of God which was given to me, as a wise master builder I have laid the foundation, and another builds on it. But let each one take heed how he builds on it. For no other foundation can anyone lay than that which is laid, which is Jesus Christ." 1 Corinthians 3:9-11 NKJV

Paul is saying, "Don't change the foundation that has been laid." I promise you, that group that denies the power of the Holy Spirit for today is changing it. They say, "Oh, that's passed away." Don't follow them, because if anyone tries to change the foundation, Paul says in Galatians 1, "If anyone changes the gospel I gave you, they are to be accursed." So, please don't follow them. He says, "Let anyone who changes it be cursed." And yet they're saying, "Well, it's changed—that was only for Paul." I'm like, 'You're cursed!' You can either repent or leave, because that's not the gospel—it's heresy, and it's leaven, and it affects the body of Christ.

How come in Africa, South America, China, and all over the world, the Church is exploding? How come last night, a thousand people probably got saved, and 600 or so the night before? You know how they do it around the world? By the gospel of the Kingdom and the name of Jesus, by the power of God. That's how they do it.

Here in the West, we're like, "We got two saved this year! It was wonderful." And it's because we've been convinced after long arguments. But we don't have to live that way, Church—we need the power of God! Paul says in 1 Corinthians 2, "I didn't come to you with lofty words, I came to you with the demonstration of the Spirit and of power." Yet this other group goes and says, "That was just for then." No! That wasn't just for then!

"For the promise is for you and your children and for all who are far off, as many as the Lord our God will call to Himself." Acts 2:39 NASB1995

Additionally, 1 Corinthians 3:11-13 says:

"For no other foundation can anyone lay than that which is laid, which is Jesus Christ. Now if anyone builds on this foundation with gold, silver, precious stones, wood, hay, straw, each one's work will become clear; for the Day will declare it, because it will be revealed by fire; and the fire will test each one's work, of what sort it is. If anyone's work which he has built on it endures, he will receive a reward. If anyone's work is burned, he will suffer loss; but he himself will be saved, yet so as through fire." 1 Corinthians 3:11-15 NKJV

What is Paul talking about? The Day of the Lord. So, denying the power of God today is building with straw, and they'll go through all their works being burned up, but they themselves will be saved. That's it though—they'll have nothing. They'll make it in, but none of their works will. What are the garments of the bride in Revelation 19? The righteous works of the saints. So, if our works aren't the righteous works of the saints, we'll get in, but we'll just be naked.

So we have to be very careful that we don't change what Jesus told us to do. What He told us to do is the silver and gold. Jesus' commands are the silver and gold. Preach the gospel of the Kingdom. Jesus says in Matthew chapter 10, He sends His disciples out. You can't get any clearer directions of what Jesus wants from His disciples than Matthew chapter 10. Every time He sends His disciples out, that's what He expects them to do, and that's what they're to do forever until He comes.

"Go preach the gospel of the Kingdom, and the name of Jesus". That's what we see in Acts chapter 8. "Heal the sick, raise the dead, cleanse the lepers, and cast out demons. Freely give what you freely received." Then He says in Mark chapter 16, "These signs will accompany those who believe: They'll cast out demons, they'll speak in new tongues, they'll tread on serpents, they'll lay their hands on the sick, and they shall recover."

This is what the believer's life should look like. Why? Because it's the Kingdom of God. If sickness doesn't belong in the Kingdom, then get it out. If demons don't belong in the Kingdom, then get them out. If the dead don't belong in the Kingdom, then raise them up. We preach the name of Jesus because it's at the name of Jesus that we are saved. But once you've entered the Kingdom, there's work to do.

He's inaugurated the Kingdom, and He will consummate it in the future. How many of you remember World War II? You probably studied it in school. We know about this event called D-Day. It was the turning point of World War II. There was a victory on the beaches of Normandy—it cost many lives, but it set the Germans on their heels, driving them back toward Berlin. D-Day was what determined the outcome of the war. The determination of how the war would end happened on that very day.

However, it wasn't V-Day—it was D-Day. V-Day wasn't for another 11 months. Did you know America lost more troops between D-Day and V-Day than they did at any point before the war? There were casualties, but V-Day was certain. And on the cross of Calvary, D-Day happened. Satan got a nail in his coffin. V-Day is determined—it is going to happen. It's not a matter of "if"—it's "when."

We have joined with God in this work to prepare for V-Day, which is coming. We don't know the hour, but it's on its way. It's certain—there's no question whether there's going to be victory on that day. The victory has been determined; we're just in this in-between period of cleanup. And we're the cleanup crew.

The King is going to sit where the enemy set up his throne—the enemy's throne will be destroyed, and the King is coming, declaring, "I am cleaning up the mess of the earth—healing the sick, raising the dead, cleansing the lepers," just like how John the Baptist was preparing the way, making straight paths for the coming of the Lord so that when He comes, it's ready for Him. The earth doesn't look like it ought to, so He sent us to go and clean it up so He can take His throne.

"You'll preach the gospel of the Kingdom to the ends of the earth, and then I will come." That's what the Scriptures tell us. He's waiting for you and me to make His coming ready. I think it's been extended many times because the Church hasn't made herself ready and prepared for the coming of the King. It could have been quick work.

But in the year 313 A.D. Christianity was legalized, and at the legalization of Christianity, a halt took place. And Christianity no longer cost anyone anything. But the original gospel said, "Deny yourself, take up your cross, and follow Me," because you already died with Christ, and you'll live forever. Now it's time to live for the Kingdom. And whether you live or die, you live in Christ. You're already living according to the future Kingdom, so now, even if they take your head off, you live, as Paul said, "To live is Christ, and to die is gain."

But because someone said, "Don't do that—don't call people to the cross. The authorities told us not to do this." We stopped keeping the pure words of God. But let me tell you—we have a higher authority than the authority of this earth. His name is Jesus. He's King, and we must obey Him. Even if they put us in jail or take our heads—I don't care. There are dying people whom Jesus paid for, and they'll never know if I follow all of the things the government says.

You know, in China, they're never free to gather like we do in America. There's actually a legal church that the government of China allows Chinese believers to have. They took all the important Scriptures out, made their own Bible, and said, "You're not allowed to talk about those things." And part of the Church said, "Okay, thank you very much." That church is not growing—that church is dead.

But the underground Church in China said, "You can put us in prison, you can take our heads, but we must preach about Jesus." You know, that's the largest Church on earth—larger than all the churches in America, all the churches in Europe combined. The Church in China alone is bigger and growing faster. Why? Because they understand the gospel of the Kingdom.

When Peter and John were told, "You stop talking about

Jesus," they said, "Who should we listen to? You or God?" The authorities responded, "Okay, alright. If you talk about Jesus again, we're going to kill you." Peter and John's response was, "Do it." They beat them and let them go. Peter and John celebrated taking stripes for Jesus. Peter and John were like, "They beat us. That's awesome! Praise God! We just gained some kind of reward in the Kingdom, I know it. We were proud to boast of Him publicly, and He says He'll be proud to boast of us before His Father." That's the good news!

Here's the secret to all of it, because there's a teeter-totter on every truth, and we need to balance the truth with the truth, having the whole counsel of God. If we don't do the work He's asked of us, He's not going to be pleased. But the other side of this truth is what we see with Mary and Martha in Luke 10. Martha's trying to do all the work, and Jesus is like, "Look, you can do that, but Mary is going to get the reward, and she's not working—she's sitting at My feet."

And what I believe is that we must be Mary first. Everything must come from sitting at His feet. We're going to do work, but may we be Mary first, and do the works from a place of abiding. There will be those on that day who say, "Didn't we cast out demons and prophesy in Your name?" And He'll say to them, "I never knew you." Why? They never sat at His feet. They didn't truly know Him. They knew how to move according to the Spirit, but they didn't know Him.

"I am the true vine, and My Father is the vinedresser. Every branch in Me that does not bear fruit He takes away; and every branch that bears fruit He prunes, that it may bear more fruit. You are already clean because of the word which I have spoken to you. Abide in Me, and I in you. As the branch cannot bear fruit of itself, unless it abides in the vine, neither can you, unless you abide in Me. I am the vine, you are the branches. He who abides in Me, and I in him,

bears much fruit; for without Me you can do nothing. If anyone does not abide in Me, he is cast out as a branch and is withered; and they gather them and throw them into the fire, and they are burned. If you abide in Me, and My words abide in you, you will ask what you desire, and it shall be done for you. By this My Father is glorified, that you bear much fruit; so you will be My disciples."
John 15:1-8 NKJV

Notice the first words: "I Am." What's the name of God the Father? "I Am." Jesus just said about Himself, "I Am." What's amazing is the Gospel of John is all formed around seven "I Am" statements. The Synoptic Gospels (Matthew, Mark, and Luke) are about understanding the Kingdom. And John's like, "Okay, you understand the Kingdom, but let me make sure you understand Jesus." And he gives the seven "I Am" statements of Jesus, and he writes the whole Gospel based on those seven "I Am" statements.

You should read John—you should read the whole thing. But, if it's not balanced by the Kingdom, it's going to be off. John invites us to wonderful intimacy with God—snuggling up against Jesus' chest. Matthew, Mark, and Luke declare, "Let's storm the gates of hell!" Somehow John's one book weighs and balances three Gospels—it's amazing.

It's very important that we balance this. If we go to John and ask the question, "Who is God?" we find that He is love. And John goes deep on Jesus, who is this God—who is love, and you'll see the word "love" a lot. But John also talks about being planted by the Lord. We read it back in Isaiah 60 and 61, where both chapters talk about us being the planted ones of the Lord to bring Him glory.

I believe that "Mary posture and attitude"—being the planted of the Lord—is what this looks like. You can't bear fruit unless you are planted of the Lord. Let's break down John 15, Jesus says,

"I am the vine, and My Father is the vinedresser. Every branch in Me that does not bear fruit, He takes away. And every branch that bears fruit, He prunes, that it may bear more fruit." John 15:1-2 NKJV

He continues:

"Abide in Me, and I in you. As the branch cannot bear fruit of itself, unless it abides in the vine, neither can you, unless you abide in Me. I am the vine, you are the branches. He who abides in Me, and I in him, bears much fruit; for without Me you can do nothing." John 15:4-5 NKJV

It's like, "Didn't He just say that?" Anytime you read something in Scripture and you think, "I'm pretty sure He just said that," He's trying to get your attention. He's saying, "This is very important—I'll say it twice."

"If anyone does not abide in Me, he is cast out as a branch and is withered; they gather them and throw them into the fire, and they are burned. If you abide in Me, and My words abide in you," John 15:6-7 NKJV

What does it look like when He abides in us and His Word abides in us?

"You will ask what you desire, and it shall be done for you. By this My Father is glorified." John 15:7-8 NKJV

Did you catch it? Isaiah 60 and 61 say He will plant you, you'll bear fruit, and you'll bring glory to the Father. Jesus just said, "I am the vine, you are the branches. My Father is the vinedresser. When you allow Him to prune you, you'll bear much fruit, and you'll bring glory to the Lord." So, all of the fruit of the Kingdom—preaching the gospel of the Kingdom, healing, raising, delivering—starts right here: 'You abide in Him.'

You want to bring God glory? Abide in Him. Abide in His Word and let His Word abide in you. You've got to have your own time to know the Word, to know the truth, so you can be free and stay free, abide, produce fruit, and bring glory to God. If you want to heal the sick, raise the dead, and cleanse the lepers. Sit at His feet, read His Word, and listen to His voice. Then healing and all the rest of that stuff is easy—we can teach you to do that in a weekend. It's really easy. He does all of it. Now, let's abide.

We must understand the gospel as a Kingdom that has a King, and us as a people preparing for the coming of that King—the King who has come and is coming. The entire New Testament is like that. Some ask, "Has He come, or is He coming?" And the New Testament answers, Yes. We must weigh it that way. We're saved by faith, but we have work to do. We get off balance when we make one greater than the other. All of it is balanced this way.

It's important that we understand that Jesus' Kingdom is both now and not yet. That's the tension we live in. The Kingdom has been inaugurated—it's here—but the full manifestation of it is still coming. That's the 'not yet' part. But as His people, we live in that in-between space where the Kingdom is breaking into this world through us.

When we abide in Him, we bear the fruit of the Kingdom in the here and now. We're called to do the work of the Kingdom, bringing healing, deliverance, and the good news to those who are lost and hurting. But we do this while keeping our eyes on the fullness of the Kingdom that is still to come. Jesus said;

"Seek first the kingdom of God and His righteousness, and all these things shall be added to you." Matthew 6:33 NKJV

What does it mean to seek the Kingdom first? It means that the Kingdom of God and His righteousness should be the central focus of our lives. Everything else—our jobs, families, and even our ministries—must come under the rule and reign of King Jesus. It's His Kingdom that we're building, not our own. We also see that in the Lord's Prayer, where Jesus taught us to pray,

"Your kingdom come, Your will be done on earth as it is in heaven." Matthew 6:10 NKJV

This is a powerful declaration that God's Kingdom would invade earth, that His will would be done here just as it is done in heaven. That means we're praying for the realities of heaven—where there is no sickness, no pain, no sorrow, and no sin—to break into our world. And this happens through us, the Church. The Church is the agent of the Kingdom on earth. We are the body of Christ, and as His body, we are called to continue His work, proclaiming the gospel of the Kingdom and demonstrating its power. Jesus gave us the Great Commission in Matthew's Gospel.

"All authority has been given to Me in heaven and on earth. Go therefore and make disciples of all the nations, baptizing them in the name of the Father and of the Son and of the Holy Spirit, teaching them to observe all things that I have commanded you; and lo, I am with you always, even to the end of the age." Matthew 28:18-20 NKJV

This commission is our mission until Jesus returns. We're called to go and make disciples—not just converts, but disciples who follow Jesus and obey His commands. We're also called to baptize them and teach them to obey everything that Jesus commanded. Notice that Jesus said, "I am with you always, even to the end of the age." This means that we're not doing this on our own. Jesus is with us, and through the power of the Holy

Spirit, we're able to accomplish this mission. But this mission is not just about preaching words—it's about demonstrating the Kingdom with power. Jesus said,

> "But you shall receive power when the Holy Spirit has come upon you; and you shall be witnesses to Me in Jerusalem, and in all Judea and Samaria, and to the end of the earth." Acts 1:8 NKJV

We can't fulfill the Great Commission without the power of the Holy Spirit. The early Church understood this. They didn't just preach the gospel—they demonstrated the power of the Kingdom. That's why we see miracles, signs, and wonders throughout the book of Acts. They weren't just words—they were a demonstration of the Kingdom. Paul said,

> "For the kingdom of God is not in word but in power." 1 Corinthians 4:20 NKJV

The Kingdom is not just about preaching or teaching—it's about demonstrating the power of God. And that power is available to every believer. Jesus didn't just send out the apostles with this mission—He sent out all of His disciples. That includes us.

> "And these signs will follow those who believe: In My name they will cast out demons; they will speak with new tongues; they will take up serpents; and if they drink anything deadly, it will by no means hurt them; they will lay hands on the sick, and they will recover." Mark 16:17-18 NKJV

These signs aren't just for a select few—they are for all believers. The power of the Holy Spirit is available to us today, just as it was for the early Church. When we understand the Kingdom and its power, we can walk in the fullness of what Jesus has called us to do. But remember, as we mentioned earlier, all of this comes from a place of abiding in Jesus. We can't do anything in our own strength. This means that everything we do in the Kingdom must come from our connection to Jesus. We must remain in Him, spending time in His presence, listening to His voice, and being led by His Spirit. That's how we bear fruit. That's how we bring the realities of the Kingdom into the world around us.

The Kingdom is here, and it's coming. We are called to live in the tension of the 'now and the 'not yet'. We proclaim the gospel of the Kingdom, we demonstrate its power, and we prepare for the day when Jesus will return and fully establish His reign on earth. Until then, we have work to do. We must be about the Father's business, bringing His Kingdom to earth and making disciples of all nations. And we do this with the assurance that Jesus is with us, and that His power is available to us through the Holy Spirit.

The day is coming when the fullness of the Kingdom will be here—when Jesus will wipe away every tear, and there will be no more death, sorrow, or pain. But until that day, we are called to be His witnesses, demonstrating His Kingdom and His power to a world that desperately needs Him. Let's live with urgency, knowing that the time is short and that the King is coming soon. Let's seek first His Kingdom and His righteousness, and trust that everything else will be added to us as we do the work He's called us to do.

Let us be the Church that Jesus intended us to be—a Church filled with His Spirit, walking in His power, and advancing His Kingdom on the earth. Let us be the people who carry the light of Christ into the darkest places, knowing that we are not alone. He is with us, empowering us every step of the way. The Bible says,

"For the earnest expectation of the creation eagerly waits for the revealing of the sons of God." Romans 8:19 NKJV

All of creation is waiting for us, the children of God, to rise up and take our place in the Kingdom. It's waiting for us to reveal the Kingdom of God on earth as it is in heaven. The world is hungry for something real, something that goes beyond words and doctrines—they are waiting to see the power of the Kingdom.

This is why we are here. This is our mission. We are not just here to exist until we die and go to heaven—we are here to bring heaven to earth, to bring the rule and reign of God into every sphere of life, and to bring people into the saving knowledge of Jesus Christ. The day is coming when every knee will bow and every tongue will confess that Jesus Christ is Lord, to the glory of God the Father (Philippians 2:10-11). But, until that day, let's live as citizens of His Kingdom, walking in His authority and proclaiming the good news of the Kingdom everywhere we go. The fields are ripe for harvest. Jesus said,

"The harvest truly is plentiful, but the laborers are few. Therefore pray the Lord of the harvest to send out laborers into His harvest."
Matthew 9:37-38 NKJV

Let us be those laborers. Let us be the ones who go out into the harvest fields, bringing in the lost, healing the sick, casting out demons, and raising the dead. Let us be the ones who carry the message of the Kingdom to the ends of the earth. There is no greater calling. There is no greater mission. And there is no greater reward than knowing that we are partnering with Jesus to bring His Kingdom to earth.

Therefore, rise up Church. Arise, shine, for your light has come! The Kingdom is at hand, and the King is coming soon. Let's be ready for His return by doing the work He has called us to do, empowered by His Spirit, and living in the fullness of His Kingdom. Jesus says,

"And behold, I am coming quickly, and My reward is with Me, to give to every one according to his work." Revelation 22:12 NKJV

Let us live with the knowledge that the King is coming soon. Let us live every day with the urgency and the passion that comes from knowing that we have been called to advance His Kingdom, proclaim His gospel, and demonstrate His power. Let's make sure that when He comes, we will hear the words, "Well done, good and faithful servant. Enter into the joy of your Lord."

We are His Kingdom people, and we have been given His Kingdom mission. Let us go out, in the power of the Holy Spirit, and fulfill that mission. Let's live as citizens of the Kingdom of God, with our eyes fixed on Jesus, the Author and Finisher of our faith, until He returns in glory to establish His Kingdom forever.

Discussion Questions

1. How does understanding the way Jesus demonstrated the Kingdom of God challenge your current approach to faith and ministry? In what practical ways can you participate in bringing the realities of heaven (healing, deliverance, miracles) to earth in your daily life?

2. What does it mean to abide in Christ, and how does this abiding empower you to bear fruit for the Kingdom? How can you cultivate a deeper intimacy with Jesus to ensure that your works are rooted in a genuine relationship with Him?

3. In light of this chapter's emphasis on the urgency of advancing the Kingdom, what steps can you take to align your priorities with God's mission? How does the concept of the 'now and not yet' Kingdom influence your perspective on the role of the Church and your personal responsibility in it?

5

THE ETHICS OF THE KINGDOM

As we have seen our focus must be the Kingdom of God. The Church as a whole in the West seems to not really understand this, so what we tend to do is preach the gospel of salvation. Now, the gospel of salvation is good. It's vital, actually, but it's a part of the Gospel of the Kingdom. It's just a part of it. We can preach the gospel of salvation and leave out the Gospel of the Kingdom. But we need to understand that the gospel Jesus preached was the Gospel of the Kingdom.

Why does the Church sometimes look so powerless? It's because they have the gospel of salvation but not the Gospel of the Kingdom. I believe we should preach the gospel Jesus preached because salvation is included in it. Instead of separating what benefits us from what costs us, we need the full gospel. What happens when we focus on the gospel of salvation alone is that people get saved, but then they just wait for eternity. There's nothing else to do. They think, "Hopefully I'm a good enough person, and I can get in." This leads Christians to live powerless lives because they don't understand that Jesus didn't just want to save them so that someday they could go to heaven. That's not the ultimate plan or purpose of God. Even when He taught us to pray, He said, "Your kingdom come, your will be done on earth as it is in heaven."

The Kingdom of God has to do with the rule and reign of God. The focus of this chapter will be on what I call the ethics of the Kingdom. Understanding this will enhance our understanding of the Kingdom and the whole Bible in its totality. I hope that by now, as you are reading this book, the Bible has made more sense than when you first began. Our friend Romeo, one of our disciples in Burkina Faso, West Africa, says, "The church in America is very interesting. They say, 'I like this part of the Bible, but I don't like that part.' Oh, I like this part. They just kind of pick and choose which parts they like and leave out certain parts."

Can I tell you Church, there should be no part of the Scriptures that we leave out. It all makes sense, and it all fits together as one story. But if we miss certain fundamental things, then we'll have to pick and choose because it won't make sense. If you have a cessationist background or mindset(meaning you believe the spiritual gifts have ceased), you're going to have a lot of conflict with the Bible. You'll have a lot of Scripture you have to jump over. Often, that's the group that thinks they have the right way. But to believe that, you have to skip about half the Bible. How can we think we have the right way when we have to skip half of the scriptures or say, "That's not important anymore?"

The focus of this chapter is the Sermon on the Mount. Jesus said, not one "tittle" (the smallest letter in the Hebrew Scriptures) will pass away until heaven and earth pass away. We know heaven and earth will pass away when Jesus brings a new heaven and a new earth, but until then, none of this will pass away. Yet we say, "It's passed away." That's contrary to the Scriptures. I want to ensure that you can read the fullness of the Scriptures and not feel conflicted. We've talked about why miracles, signs, and wonders followed Jesus. I hope it's blessed you to understand that Jesus didn't do miracles, signs, and wonders because He was God. He did them because in the Kingdom of God, as described in Revelation 21 and 22, those things (sickness, death, demonic oppression) don't belong there. So if Jesus is bringing His Father's Kingdom, the sick need to be healed because sickness doesn't belong in the Kingdom, demons need to be cast out because they don't belong in the Kingdom. The dead need to be raised because there's no death in the reign and rule of God. These are signs that the Kingdom is at hand.

But, there's something else we must deal with concerning the Kingdom that will change every aspect of your life: You won't just do miracles. There will be a day when Jesus says, in Matthew 7 (part of the Sermon on the Mount), that people will say, "Lord, Lord," and what will He say? Not everyone who calls out "Lord, Lord" will enter the Kingdom of Heaven. He says there will be some who do that, but His response will be, "Away from me, you workers of lawlessness, I never knew you." And they're going to say, "But we prophesied, and we did mighty wonders, and we cast out devils. Didn't we do all of this in Your name?" But He will say, "I never knew you." There's no question that you can do the works of the Kingdom, but with a key ingredient missing, Jesus will say, "I don't know you." This is why this chapter is so important.

Jesus prays in John 17, which is really the Lord's Prayer, because it's when the Lord prayed. We like to call the prayer in Matthew 6, where Jesus teaches the disciples to pray, the Lord's Prayer. He says, "Don't pray long, repetitious prayers like the Gentiles do, thinking they'll be heard for their many words. Don't pray like that." They would chant, like what witches do. He said, "Don't pray like that. Pray like this: Our Father, who art in heaven..." We call this the Lord's Prayer, but Jesus actually had a prayer that was His prayer, the Lord's prayer, and in that intimate moment with the Father, He prayed something else:

> *"That they all may be one, as You, Father, are in Me, and I in You; that they also may be one in Us, that the world may believe that You sent Me." John 17:21 NKJV*

A few verses later Jesus reveals that this is His desire. The desire of Jesus, who has no other desires except the Father's desires, shows that this is what the Father desires. It's that we all would be one together, and that we would be one with Him, who is one with the Father in the Spirit. This is the actual goal of the Father, Son, and Holy Spirit—that we would have what they have, which is this beautiful harmony in their relationship.

Now, this is not easy. It's actually very difficult. If you are married, you understand this. How many of you have found difficulties in marriage? Yet it's the desire of God for us to become one in our marriage, right? And the desire of Jesus is that His church would be one, and that she would be one with Him. The world would respond by saying, "Wow, we want that." There's a oneness God is after in His church—not the kind of oneness that comes from having a written certificate of marriage, but the oneness of a life lived and experienced, of growth and maturity, where our lives are knit together, so that God Himself would look and say, "Wow, they are one."

Even with your children, you and your household, that there'd be oneness. Even with your neighbors, that there would be oneness. This is the desire of God. I know here in the US we are called the "United States," but I also know there's a lot of conflict and division, which is not the desire of God. Jesus' desire is that we would be one.

The Scriptures in the Old Testament give us a way to be right with God, to be one with God. It's the law. God gave the law. In Exodus chapter 20, He gave the Ten Commandments. "If you do this, then you'll be righteous," meaning you'll be in right standing with God. And at the end of this life, if you've done all these things, you'll be right with God and you'll receive eternal life. This is how the Old Testament was. But, Jesus comes and says, "I haven't come to do away with that. I've come to fulfill it." (Matthew 5:17)

The way they would have lived was works-based: If I do this, then I get this. But Jesus flips it. There's this thing called an imperative: "You are." Then there's an indicative: "the result of what you are." For example, let's use a dog. Let's say you are a dog, and dogs fetch balls. Being a dog is the imperative, and fetching balls is the indicative. So a dog fetches balls because it is a dog. In the Old Testament, the imperative came after the indicative: If you live righteously, if you obey the law, then you'll be righteous, you'll be blessed, and you'll get eternal life. In the New Testament, the imperative comes first: "You are righteous." The indicative comes after: "Live righteously."

If we don't get this, we'll live religiously. We'll live doing godly things so that we can get something. The New Testament says, "You have it, so live it." The imperative comes first, so the indicative comes after. I want to show you this in Matthew chapter 5 because this is vital to understanding Christianity. You cannot be righteous on your own. Your indicative will never make your imperative. It will never work that way. You'll never become a child of God because of your good efforts. Some of us are working really hard to be good, and it's exhausting. If that's you, I'm excited for you to understand this revelation: Let the imperative come first. Let it be declared about you so that you can live out the result of it. ***You are a child of God.***

The Sermon on the Mount is an imagery of Jesus being the greater Moses, the one greater than Moses. Moses said, "One is coming who is like me but greater. He'll be a prophet like me, but He'll be greater."(Deuteronomy 18:18). Jesus, in the Sermon on the Mount, goes up on a mountain. Where did Moses get the law? On a mountain. So Jesus is playing this out. He goes up, has them sit down, and He begins to give them the law—but in a different way. The imperative comes first. He says, "Blessed!" You are blessed, so let's go through it quickly:

"Blessed are the poor in spirit..." Matthew 5:3 NKJV

The imperative comes first: You're blessed, so you are poor in spirit. "Blessed" is what you are; what you do comes after what you are. You are blessed, and because of that, you're poor in spirit.

- "Blessed are those who mourn, for they shall be comforted."
- "Blessed are the meek, for they shall inherit the earth."
- "Blessed are those who hunger and thirst for righteousness, for they shall be filled."

And on it goes. I would encourage everyone to spend time reading in the scriptures what I'm talking about in this chapter because there is so much to it. The imperative comes first: **You are blessed**, and the blessed are like this. Jesus goes on to say,

"You are the salt of the earth." Matthew 5:13 NKJV

You are—this is what you are. The imperative comes first. Then He says, "You are the light of the world. Let your light shine." The imperative of what you are—light—releases the indicative of you shining out because of what you are. You are the light, so you shine. You are salt, so be salty. You are blessed, and this is what that's like. This messes with the Pharisees because they're trying to earn something, and Jesus is flipping it: *You are* going to be like this because this is who you are. If you flip it over, you'll go back to religion and try to earn it. Jesus declares, "You are righteous; now live righteously." This changes everything. This messes with those who understand the law in the New Testament era. But this is what Jesus goes on to say;

> *"Do not think that I came to destroy the Law or the Prophets. I did not come to destroy but to fulfill. For assuredly, I say to you, till heaven and earth pass away, one jot or one tittle will by no means pass from the law till all is fulfilled." Matthew 5:17-18 NKJV*

Until we come fully into it, He says, "Whoever therefore breaks one of the least of these commandments and teaches others to do the same shall be called the least" (verse 19).

> *"For I say to you, that unless your righteousness exceeds the righteousness of the scribes and Pharisees, you will by no means enter the kingdom of heaven." Matthew 5:20 NKJV*

For the Jewish people—the fishermen, tax collectors, and the normal everyday people listening—they must have thought, "How can we do that? Unless it goes beyond their righteousness?" They're thinking, "Who can get in, then?" Jesus is the only one who by His own effort and work can get in.

Let me solve something for you that's difficult for theologians. This is a big issue for Reformed churches. They don't want repentance to be a work because the Scripture says in Ephesians 2:8, "We are saved by grace through faith, not of our own doing, lest we boast." So, we're not saved by our works. This is the issue: People don't want repentance to be a work because in the Scriptures, faith and repentance go together. If they do, then you're working. To avoid this, people don't call for repentance. But that's not the case. It's not complicated.

How do we get in? By faith. Where does faith come from? Hearing the word of God. When you hear the word of God, there's something on it—it's grace. When you hear it, it's the rhema of God, not just the logos. The logos is the written word of God; rhema is the freshly spoken word of God. When we speak the logos with the Spirit of God, it becomes rhema. And when you hear it, you say, "Oh my gosh, this is true!" Grace made you able to see what you couldn't see before. You believe—it's faith-based. Now, because you believe, there's a work to do that you couldn't do before without grace.

What is grace? This is where the Church struggles. Grace is divine empowerment—God giving you the power to do something you can't do. You're saved by His power, not yours. Not by might, not by power, but by His Spirit. So yes, we do need to repent, and there is work to be done.

"For we are His workmanship, created in Christ Jesus for good works, which God prepared beforehand that we should walk in them." Ephesians 2:10 NKJV

There are good works to do that we couldn't do in our own power. So yes, repentance is a work, but it's not a work of your power. It's a work of His grace. Grace empowers you to see that you're going the wrong direction, and by His power you turn and go the right way. Repentance is the turning away. You were going one way, and Ephesians 2 talks about this: You were once like the Gentiles, going your own way according to the prince of the power of the air, a son of destruction. But because of His grace, you see that Jesus is the Son of God, and He's going this way. Grace makes you able to turn and follow Him.

Your repentance—your response of turning away from going your way to go His way—was because His grace made you able to see and gave you the power to turn. So, there is work to do, but you can't do it on your own. Not by your might or strength, but by His grace. That's why you are blessed—you have His grace. You're blessed. When you believe because you heard the word of

God and His grace was on it, you have faith. The Bible says that in that moment, you became a child of God. To all who believe, He has given the right to become children of God. In that moment, God is for you, and you are blessed because His grace has come. He's given you life and the ability to walk the right way.

What happens is you start to mourn because of your sin. You have a revelation that you've been sinning. You were living a certain way in the world, and you didn't have any conviction about it. This is how I was: I robbed people. I thought, "Oh, you have this and I don't, but I want it, so I'll take it and you can try doing something about it." I did all kinds of crazy stuff. Then I got saved and thought, "What am I doing? I can't do this anymore." My friends thought, "Hey, come with me, go this way," and I said, "I can't go that way. I can't do that anymore." Something inside me didn't want to do that. I just said, "No, thank you."

When certain things came out of my mouth, I'd think, "What was that? It's disgusting. I don't like it anymore." That was His grace inside me, witnessing that I'm a child of God, transforming me, granting me repentance, and bearing witness that I'm alive now. He says, "Those who follow Him, who walk by the Spirit, are God's children."

This is another issue the Church has: We've believed this lie that says, "I believe that I'm a child of God, and that's it, so I just wait for heaven one day and don't really need to change much." No. He says, "Those who walk according to the Spirit—those are the children of God." You'll find that in Romans, Ephesians, Galatians—over and over. Those who live according to the Spirit don't gratify the flesh. Those who live according to the flesh are dead, because the wages of sin is death, and the flesh only produces sin. But we don't do that anymore because we're the children of God. We walk according to the Spirit.

Gordon Fee, an amazing theologian and one of my favorite people, said, "A Christian is someone who really wants to be one." That's my definition of a Christian: someone who really wants to be one. Meaning, you have this desire to do what's right. But for those who say, "I believe, and I know God says don't do this, don't do that, but." And His voice doesn't convict them at all, and they don't hunger and thirst for righteousness—are they really a child of God? You are a child of God. You are blessed. You're blessed when you hunger and thirst for righteousness—it's the result of what you are.

A Christian is someone who really wants to be one. Someone who really wants righteousness, who really wants God, who really wants to walk in the light, who really wants to be free. That's what a Christian is—those who are going to seek first His Kingdom and His righteousness. Now, we must remember, we can't do it in our own strength. We get it by His Spirit, His strength, His power.

I want to hone in on three things: love, humility, and honor. Jesus, in the second half of Matthew chapter 5, goes through the second half of the Ten Commandments. The first half of the Ten Commandments is about righteousness between you and God. The second half is about righteousness between you and man. The first half says, don't have idols, don't have other gods, don't worship or blaspheme the Lord's name. These all concern loving God. The second half concerns the relationship between you and your neighbor. This is how the law is—that's why loving God and loving your neighbor fulfills the whole law, because it's concerning God and your neighbor. (Matthew 22:37-40, Romans 13:8-10)

To break this down, Jesus is doing this in Matthew chapters 5 through 7. Jesus also adds some things. Chapter 6 of Matthew is all about righteousness with God—how you pray, how you fast, and how you give. Don't do it for man, do it for God. You'll do it in secret because God knows what you do in secret, and He will reward you publicly. Then He talks about possessions—how you relate to possessions now because of who you are. Jesus is redefining your relationship to possessions, showing how you relate to the world and the material things of the world because of who you are. To recap: Jesus explains how you relate to God, how you relate to your neighbor, and how you relate to the possessions of the world. These are all covered in the Sermon on the Mount because He's re-giving the law through the lens of the Spirit.

Now, I want to give you three things. Jesus says, do this one thing and you'll fulfill it all. A lot of times, we think, "I want to do that, but I don't fully know how," and we miss the other two things that are a result of this. If we can see all three, we'll be able to do it. Let me show you three things that result in God's desire. Again, God's desire is for us to be one. This is His eternal desire. This is why this is important, because you're not going to heal the sick in eternity. You're not going to cast out devils in eternity. But you will do what I'm talking about today in eternity. What did Jesus say fulfills the law? Love.

The first thing is love. If you understand love, the law will be easy. One of the commands is, "Don't commit adultery." The Pharisees were like, "Yeah, I've never done that. I'm good." But did you know that you could be a wretch and not commit adultery? So that doesn't really accomplish God's desire.

We can have this "boundary" where we think, as long as I don't go outside of this law, I'm good—but you could still be a wretch inside it. He says, "Don't murder." You know, you could be a wretch and not murder. Jesus says, "If you lust for your neighbor's wife or husband if you even have it in your heart like you wish you could, you've already done it." It starts in the heart.

It all begins in the heart. He takes the law and applies it to your heart. Where does the Kingdom of God start? The Pharisees wanted to know when, how and where the Kingdom of God would come. Jesus said in Luke 17, "It's inside you." The reign and rule of God begins inside you. So does sin.

Jesus says murder starts with hatred. We could say, "I'm righteous because I haven't murdered," and Jesus says, "Let me give you a new definition of righteousness: Don't have any hate in your heart toward your brother." Because the goal is connection with your brother. Can you not murder your brother and still live disconnected? We've already failed then, because God's goal is connection—it's oneness.

If I have someone in my life and every time I see them, I think, 'I can't stand them. I can't stand what they wear. They think they're so special.' But I haven't killed them, so I must still be righteous. Jesus is like, 'That's not how this works. Let me help you understand what I came to really do.'

Jesus even talks about not greeting someone. He said, when you only greet your family and those you like, what good is that? If you see someone you know has wronged you, whatever it is, and you just act like you don't see them—that's not God's way. Maybe you see them in the grocery store, but you pretend like you didn't. You just walk right by them. But you'd be so excited if you saw your second-grade teacher, someone you absolutely loved, "Oh, Mrs. Potts, what's up? You remember me?" You're so excited to see them. But with that other person, you'd just keep your head down and find a different aisle. Jesus says, 'you've already missed my desire, which is oneness.'

The goal isn't just to not murder or not commit adultery. The goal is that you would have connection through sincere love. If we don't have that, we've already fallen short of God's desire. That's why in marriage, we think we're doing good because we haven't divorced. But if we don't have love and connection, we've already failed.

This puts the bar so high that we think, "I need God." Yes, we do. The Pharisees thought they had it without God, but Jesus turns it around so people realize, "Oh, we need God." Exactly! You can't do this in your own strength—not by might, not by power. This is where you actually need God. You must first know who you are, that you're loved and chosen—not because of your good works, but because of His. I think these three things—love, humility, and honor—are a three-strand cord. They will produce connection. The goal is oneness with God and with your neighbor, in your marriage, with your kids, and in all your relationships. That's the goal. But you're going to need these three ethics or character traits that make up the culture of the Kingdom to achieve it: love, humility, and honor—in that order.

First, I must be connected to Love Himself, the source of love. Jesus says, "Abide in Me, for apart from Me you can do no good thing." You can't do any good work if you're not abiding in Him. Listen, I've been following the Lord for over two decades, and I'm telling you, I've devoured the Bible. I cannot get enough. I pray, I spend time with God and do all this stuff. But if I were to walk away from my relationship with the Lord for a season, or if He removed His grace for a moment, I would be hours or days away from being the worst sinner I know.

This is how I know: If I see a donut, my eyes and flesh start drawing all my attention and affection to it. If on my own I don't have the power or strength to overcome donuts, then without His grace, I'd be like that with a million other things. How many of you know people like that? They get one thing, but it's not enough, so they need something else.

This is what I told one of my friends. I said, "Man, I know you're going after getting this house and this and that, but the house isn't going to be enough." He wasn't a believer yet. I said, "In about a year, you'll say, 'This house isn't big enough.' Then you'll have a kid on the way. After your second kid, you'll say, 'I need something bigger.' And so you'll get that one. Then you'll have the space, but you'll think, 'These countertops, man. I need granite.' It's just never going to be enough. And that truck you have with big tires, it's lifted, blows smoke when you hit the gas, turbo and all... It's just not going to be enough. One day, you'll look at it and think, 'It doesn't blow enough smoke, it doesn't go fast enough. It's just not enough.'"

That's how we are apart from God. In Genesis 11, men were building cities, and they thought, "Let's build a tower for our sake and our name." This is humanity. Why do we do all this? Somehow, it gratifies something—how people think of us. When people go on vacation, they post a photo. Someone needs to be jealous of how great our lives are. Now, I'm not saying it's wrong to post a photo, but what's the motive? We have to get to the heart of the issue.

This corruption in man's heart says, "I need your approval. I need your praise. It makes me feel something." But when we are satisfied with God, we won't think that way. Someone will get something better than you, and you'll celebrate with them. You'll praise God for it because your heart is already captivated and fulfilled in Him.

We must first come under the fountain of His love and abide there. If we remove the fountain of His love, we'll start noticing thoughts in our hearts like, "I did all this for you, and you didn't do anything back. You didn't say thank you. You didn't..." You'll start focusing on what people didn't do, or what you think God didn't do and you'll be focused on what you think you did and how you should be treated because of it.

Why? Because your love tank is emptying, and you're not staying connected to the fountain of His love. We blame God: "I poured out, and You didn't pour back in." But that's what a corrupted heart does: "I'm going to keep a record of what you owe me." But if we stay connected to the fountain of love, love keeps no record of wrongs. Why? Because it's too focused on Who God is and what He's done. You're overwhelmed by His goodness, and you don't even notice.

If I'm not satisfied, I'm going to find someone who should be helping satisfy me, so they're now my bad guy. We have to be satisfied with God and find satisfaction in Him. If we're being satisfied by watching stuff online, by purchasing things, by going on shopping sprees, or whatever it is, it's because we're not being satisfied where we ought to be. And all that stuff will rust and disappear. That's what the Scriptures are saying: Put your treasure in God, where there's no rust, nothing to destroy.

The second thing is humility. Here's how you can be humble: The opposite of humility is pride. How much does God hate pride? A lot. God opposes the proud but gives grace to the humble. So, we need grace—that's how we do all this. Did you know that understanding how much you are loved, and the depths to which God went to show you His love, will actually produce humility in you? Realizing how much God forgave you and how great a sinner you were will produce something in you. Jesus says, "Those who have been forgiven much, love much."

The only reason we struggle to forgive someone else is because we think we deserve forgiveness. But, if we never forget that it was only by His grace, only by His mercy—that we deserved hell, but He was merciful—it will produce mercy, love, and humility in our hearts. If someone else does something wrong, we'll remember, "Yeah, I've done that too." If someone's acting outside of their created identity and it hurts, unforgiveness won't even cross your mind because you remember, "I've been there too."

Never forget the mercy God showed you and that the only reason you're right with God, the only reason you have anything good in your life, is because of His mercy and grace. That will humble you.

This is why we can't earn salvation, being right with God, or eternal life. If we could, we'd be proud of it. And pride is not the nature or character of God—it's the opposite. If we think we can have all this because we're good, we've missed it. No, I was a wretch, and He was good. He gave me mercy. So, you humble yourself. You have a proper view of yourself.

C. S. Lewis said, "Humility is not thinking less of yourself; it's thinking of yourself less." So you don't think, "I'm just a wretched sinner." No, no, no. *I was, but I'm not.* That's not who I am anymore. I was, but now I'm not, and it's only because of His grace. That's how we must view it. If you never forget how much He paid to forgive you, you'll remember that others need forgiveness too. It's in your heart to give it because you've received so much.

It's hard for me to relate to people who say, "I just can't forgive them." I think, "Whatever happened to you has most likely happened to me too." We need to see through the lens of Christ. You know when people talk about seeing the world through rose-colored glasses? I call my lens the crimson glasses. Once you put on crimson glasses, which represent the blood of Jesus, you view people through the blood of Jesus. Jesus doesn't view you through your sin; He views you through the blood. The Father doesn't view you through your sin; He views you through the blood. I can't afford to have a thought in my mind about you that God doesn't have about you. The only way to do that is to view people through the blood of Jesus.

This takes us to the third part, honor: When we look at people, we have to start valuing people, because honor has to do with value. But what happens is we don't want to value certain people because of their actions. But people are no longer valued by their actions—they're valued by the blood of Jesus. This will change everything.

Let's say someone does something to me. But I don't view them by their actions—why? Whose image were they made in, and by whose blood were they purchased? God thinks they're worth His own blood, His own life. The highest price ever paid on this earth was the blood of Jesus, and He poured it out to purchase them. So that's what they're worth. Their actions don't define their worth—the blood of Jesus does. I can understand that they're not living up to their value, and love always lifts people up to their value.

So I'm not going to avoid them; I'm going to move toward them with compassion to help them live according to their value. Not get frustrated and think, "Oh, that person." No, they're just living short of what God wants for them, and they need help.

This is the three-strand cord of love, humility, and honor that Jesus taught and modeled. Let me share something powerful about honor. We understand the principle of sowing and reaping: God says, "whatever you sow, you shall also reap." (Galatians 6:7) No one sows without the intent of reaping. That's foolishness; it's bad stewardship. You sow with the purpose of reaping what you sow. But there's something greater than this and it's called inheritance, where you reap what you didn't sow. And inheritance is accessed through honor.

What you sow is honor, and what you reap is what's on their life. The only way in the Scriptures to receive an inheritance is through honor. The Lord says,

> *"Honor your father and your mother, that your days may be long upon the land which the Lord your God is giving you." Exodus 20:12 NKJV*

Honor the Father and the Son, and you will receive eternal life. It's inheritance. We are co-heirs with Christ. The way into the Kingdom is through honor. You see Jesus for who He is, you honor that, and you get an inheritance. As Jesus said,

> *"He who receives a prophet in the name of a prophet shall receive a prophet's reward; and he who receives a righteous man in the name of a righteous man shall receive a righteous man's reward." Matthew 10:41 NASB1995*

Jesus comes as a prophet, the Word of God. We honor that, and we get an inheritance. Do you know what co-heirs mean? His inheritance is your inheritance, but you didn't get it by your work —you got it by His work. You inherited what He earned, which is eternal life. So the only way you came into the Kingdom was through honor. You recognized Jesus' value, who He really was— the Son of God—and you believed. You honored Him as such, and you reaped His work. You inherited life eternally.

Let me tell you something: You have all of something, but not all of everything. And this is why you need honor. You have all of the Father's love, but there are other things you need in this life. He doesn't give you everything. He gives you all His love. He gives all of us some things. In Ephesians 4, He says, one faith, one baptism, one Lord, one Spirit etc. Then He says, according to the grace He gave you. So not everyone is the same. He says, "You're all one," but you're not all the same, because He gave different graces—apostles, prophets, evangelists, pastors, and teachers.

So you have all of something (love), but not all of everything. The only way to get it is through honor, and the only way you'll honor is if you view yourself properly and view others properly. That comes through humility. The only way to walk in the fullness of this is to know who you are and to humble yourself, because you'll make mistakes. You'll veer off the path of following the Spirit at times, because you're learning how to walk by the Spirit. You're a child of God, and children must grow and mature. You're learning, and it's a process. God gives you the grace to come back and try again.

But if you go and hide, you won't humble yourself, because you're afraid of what people will say. So you hide your mistakes and deeds instead of exposing them, as Scripture says. You're a child of God—you no longer have to hide. The only way to expose them is through humility. This is what we say in our School of Ministry: Humility is the number one thing in walking toward freedom. Humble yourself. Number two, honesty. Expose the works of darkness in your own life. Expose them. He says we are the children of light, so walk in the light. Those who say they've never sinned are liars, Scripture says.

The way you fulfill the first and second commandments is through love, but you'll need these other two things: humility and honor. Never forget the price that was actually paid and what your transgressions, iniquities, and sins were and how God treated you in the midst of them. Treat others likewise—we're supposed to be like our Father.

Let me tell you what your Heavenly Father is like: The Scriptures say He was the husband, and Israel was the bride. He had a prophet(Hosea) stand in His position and say, "Marry that woman, Gomer. She's like Israel." When he married her, she went off and slept with other people. God told the prophet, "Go and bring her back, even though she left you." This happens again. At the end, when she has no more worth—no one wants to buy her as a prostitute anymore; they want to buy her as a servant, maybe to sweep and clean—her value as a prostitute is gone. She's been used up. Now, she's only worth being a servant, and God says, "Go get her."

That's what your Father is like when you feel like Gomer, when you feel like you've gone away, or maybe when you feel like you're married to Gomer—someone who's done pornography or worse. We're supposed to be like our Father. What does your Father do and say? "Go get her." Think about the Good Samaritan story in the context of your enemy. The one in the ditch and the one who comes to help the one who was treated poorly. I've been treated poorly many times, but the bar God set for me was: "Tom, you were once the one in the ditch, and I pulled you out. Don't walk on by—even your enemy, the one who treated you that way. Pull them out." This is what God is like. This is what Jesus was like. He was treated as a Samaritan, as a dog, by the very people He was dying for, and He says, "Forgive them, Father."

What about the Father? Maybe you're struggling with your kids. Maybe with your parents. Look at the prodigal son's story and the Father's embrace. This is what God is like, and Jesus says this is what the law is like. There's a new law.

"Bear one another's burdens, and so fulfill the law of Christ."
Galatians 6:2 NKJV

The law of Christ is love. But we have to remember what love did for us. We were once Gomer. We were once the one in the ditch. We were once the prodigal. Every time we were on the bad side, the Father was on the other side, doing us good every time.

He says, "Now, do likewise." Maybe you need to spend time repenting and turning away from your sin. You've been the one on the auction block. You've been the one in the ditch. You've been the one who's gone away, and the Father is saying, "I receive you back." Accept His hand of mercy to pull you out.

If you have people in your life that you don't want to talk to, He's saying, "Extend your hand." He says, If you're at the altar, bringing an offering, and you remember you don't have connection with someone, and you're choosing to be okay with that—leave your offering. Go and be reconciled, and then come and bring your offering. I've repented to people who others would think need to repent to me because I have a part to play in it. I'm not going to look at their part—I'm going to look at mine.

This isn't easy. We're going to need God's grace. Don't say you're a child of God and not live like one. He says,

"But if you do not forgive men their trespasses, neither will your Father forgive your trespasses." Matthew 6:15 NKJV

Unity comes when the other person repents, but forgiveness is already in your heart, ready to be used. I'm not saying if someone is doing something wrong that you should throw yourself into the situation if they're not repentant. The Father already has forgiveness in His heart toward His children, but He's also reaching out. So, we need to have forgiveness in our heart and reach out. They have to reach back with repentance.

It's easy to say, difficult to do but His grace is enough. We have to learn how to set boundaries according to the Kingdom in order to bring the response of the Kingdom, which is reconciliation. He wants you to be an ambassador of His Kingdom as a minister of reconciliation. Let's ask God for grace. You need grace; I need grace to be a person who forgives seventy times seven. To be someone who runs into the light, even though we're scared. What's going to happen? What will people say? Don't worry about that—it's about the Father. Don't worry about people; hunger and thirst for righteousness. Don't worry about how people will respond to what you did in darkness. The Father has His arms wide open. You need grace.

Pray with me: *Heavenly Father, I ask you to grant me an abundance of grace, I need your grace. I need it to forgive, to love, to walk and stay humble, I need it to be a person of honor and live honorably. Weave the three strand cord of love, humility and honor into my life and character. Be gracious to me and make your face shine upon me. Lead me by your spirit and fill me with your peace. May you bless us and keep us Lord, In Jesus' name, amen.*

Discussion Questions

1. How does shifting your focus from the gospel of salvation to the Gospel of the Kingdom change your understanding of your role and purpose as a believer? In what ways can embracing the Gospel of the Kingdom empower you to live a more active and impactful Christian life?

2. What does it mean to you that Jesus declares us righteous first, and how does this affect your approach to living righteously? How can recognizing the imperative before the indicative help you rely more on God's grace rather than your own efforts?

3. What practical steps can you take to demonstrate love, humility, and honor in your relationships to foster unity and connection? Are there specific areas or relationships in your life where practicing forgiveness or valuing others as God does is challenging? How might the principles discussed in this chapter help you address these challenges?

6

THE THRONE OF THE KINGDOM

I truly believe that our lives would look like the New Testament if we understood that we are in a kingdom, and that we have a King. We've had a Kingdom of Darkness reigning and ruling over us. People say, "If God is good, then how come bad things happen and people die?" I'm saying, the kingdom of darkness is both how and why. Darkness is real, and it's a real kingdom.

God made a good earth, and He said it was good. He created man in His likeness and He enjoyed fellowship and communion with man. He saw that man was alone and He said that wasn't good. Therefore, He gave man a beautiful wife and they walked naked through the earth together. No shame. Just enjoying themselves. I don't know about you, but that sounds like a good earth. I'd be thinking, "This is amazing!".

Then Satan came, that little liar. He began to lie and to get Adam and Eve to look at things and see them his way, contrary to the way God sees them. He began to plant seeds of doubt—maybe God wasn't as good as He seemed. Maybe He was holding something back from them. Maybe there was more goodness that God wasn't really giving them. Satan suggested that if they followed his way, they would find the good that God was keeping back from them.

He pointed at a tree that God said not to touch—the tree of the knowledge of good and evil—saying, "God knows that you'll be like Him if you eat from this." They were already like Him; God made them in His likeness. But they listened to that voice, and we get into trouble when we listen to the wrong voice. They inclined their ears to the wrong voice and began to perceive that what Satan said was true because they weren't listening to the voice of truth.

Be careful who you listen to—be careful. Because even those who walked with God—Adam and Eve, who physically walked with God upon the earth—could hear Him coming, yet they could still be deceived and go the wrong way. Be careful of who and what you listen to. There is leaven in it.

They took from the tree, and it caused something to happen: death entered the world. The Bible says the consequence of sin is death. Death entered the world, and this curse of death has come upon all humanity. The reason for all the wickedness, hurt, pain, and trauma in our lives is the kingdom of Satan and darkness. But, God began to whisper about a King who would come and put an end to that kingdom. Creation has been waiting for a King, and that King's name is God—Yahweh.

God would become our King again—King over those He made in His likeness. Those that He loves and that He said were good. He said, "I'm going to make it good again. I'm going to put an end to the terror of darkness, and I'm going to bring My goodness into the earth again."

Israel becomes the people through whom God brings this promise. He says to Abraham, "I'm going to bless you so that all nations will be blessed through you." He goes to the Israelites in Egypt and draws them out. He gives them their own land, saying, "This is going to be so good. I will bring you back into a garden flowing with milk and honey." But, when they go into the land they do it again. They turn away from God, following the way of the serpent—Satan—and they begin to oppress, abuse, and do things their way. God wasn't really King to them yet.

They said, "Give us a king who will rule over us." God's thinking, "I thought I was your King." Samuel felt rejected, but God said, "They're not rejecting you, Samuel. They're rejecting Me once more." So, God gave them over to their desire, letting them have it their way.

Man still hadn't learned that man wasn't good at reigning. God says, "I'll give you over to your own reign." The outcome was sin, death, and evil, leading back to bondage. Babylon took them away, just like Egypt did, and put them in chains. This is what the reign of humanity looks like when a man is in charge—sin, death, and evil—because of corrupted hearts.

But God continued to whisper about the coming One, the anointed King, who would take the earth and reign over it. His reign would be a reign of justice, love, mercy, and kindness. Then Jesus shows up. We read the genealogy of the people who gave birth to this person who is now a baby in a manger. How can a King be born in a trough? What kind of King is this? He's a humble one—a meek King. He won't come like the human kings who exalt themselves over people. No, He's going to exalt Himself over death so that He can exalt us back to our rightful place with Him.

This is the King who came to the earth to save His people from their sins, from death, and from decay. The Bible says in Romans chapter 3 that all have sinned and fallen short of God's glorious standard. Could it possibly be that God would look upon us and bring us into the level of intimacy that He wanted? How could it be?

I want to talk to you in this chapter about the cross—about what Jesus did for you, the cost of communion with Christ. What really happened on the cross?

> *"Let us therefore come boldly to the throne of grace, that we may obtain mercy and find grace to help in time of need." Hebrews 4:16 NKJV*

This is the desire that all of us have in our hearts. We want to come to the throne of God. It's a throne of grace—that's the throne of our God. He said, "Let us therefore come boldly to the throne of grace." This ties into the question, "If God can't look upon sin, how could it be that I could come to the throne of grace and ask for mercy?"

> *"He made Him who knew no sin to be sin for us, that we might become the righteousness of God in Him." 2 Corinthians 5:21 NKJV*

I read Leviticus 16, and things begin to make sense. There would be a priest who would take a lamb, and they would place the sin of Israel on the lamb. They would lay their hands and impart, or impute, the iniquity, transgression, and sin of the nation upon this animal, and then they would kill it. The priest would dip his hand in the blood and sprinkle it seven times over the mercy seat on the top of the ark of the covenant, which was God's throne. He would sprinkle it seven times to atone for the sin placed on the animal.

Because sin leads to death, someone has to die. They placed the sin on this lamb and took its life, and the lamb's purity was imparted to them. There is an exchange—sin gets placed on this one so that righteousness can be placed on that one. Sin was placed on Jesus. He who knew no sin had sin placed upon Him so that we might become the righteousness of God. Oh my—Jesus is King! What kind of King? A servant King, one who would die for His people.

"You are worthy to take the scroll and to open its seals, for You were slain, and have redeemed us to God by Your blood out of every tribe and tongue and people and nation, and have made us kings and priests to our God, and we shall reign on the earth." Revelation 5:9-10 NKJV

Do you see what happened? We once reigned with God. We gave our reign over to Satan, and Satan reigned. Do you want to know what Satan's reign looks like? The darkest, worst possible things you see in the earth—the things you wish were gone. That's what his reign looks like. All the good things are coming down from heaven—from God—and every dark and wicked thing comes from Satan.

There's wickedness in this earth that's beyond imagining. For example, in Nazi Germany, they would take babies and throw them out of windows of two-story or three-story buildings. They would take babies and chuck them out the windows, and people would watch their children die on the ground. That's the wickedness of Satan possessing people. It's beyond fathoming how wicked Satan is. That's what his kingdom looks like—it's so dark and terrible that you can't imagine it. It's so terrible that I wouldn't want to be here if the kingdom of darkness didn't end.

That was the kingdom that was going to possess me forever —until Jesus. Until Jesus came, this was going to be the reign of the earth. Unless God came to take the earth back, and He would have to die to do it. Someone had to pay for sin. The animal sacrifices weren't what was pleasing to God. That every year a sacrifice had to happen—sacrifice after sacrifice, death after death—was not what He wanted. He wanted life. Why? Because God doesn't want death over and over again—He wants life.

"our great God and Savior Jesus Christ, who gave Himself for us, that He might redeem us from every lawless deed and purify for Himself His own special people, zealous for good works." Titus 2:13-14 NKJV

He redeemed us—not to be zealous for the kingdom of darkness—but to be zealous for good. He has redeemed us from every lawless thing and purified us as a people for Himself, a people who love what is good.

"Let the redeemed of the Lord say so, whom He has redeemed from the hand of the enemy." Psalm 107:2 NKJV

We must declare it: I once was in the hand of the enemy, but Someone struck His hand and said, "Not today, Satan!" And then that Someone had His own hands struck to free us from the enemy's hand. He freed me from the hand of the enemy. I am the redeemed of the Lord! We are the redeemed of the Lord!

"Thus says the Lord, who created you, O Jacob, and He who formed you, O Israel: Fear not, for I have redeemed you; I have called you by your name; you are Mine." Isaiah 43:1 NKJV

Satan, you don't get to have this one. "You are Mine," the Lord says. He has redeemed you.

"I will deliver you from the hand of the wicked, And I will redeem you from the grip of the terrible." Jeremiah 15:21 NKJV

"I will ransom them from the power of the grave; I will redeem them

from death. O Death, I will be your plagues! O Grave, I will be your destruction! Pity is hidden from My eyes." Hosea 13:14 NKJV

He says, "I'm going to redeem you from death, and Death, I will be your demise." Oh, what a King! Death once ruled over us until a new King came to rule. Death tried to rule over Him, but it wasn't powerful enough. Oh, what a King!

"Do you not know that to whom you present yourselves slaves to obey, you are that one's slaves whom you obey, whether of sin leading to death, or of obedience leading to righteousness?" Romans 6:16 NKJV

Whoever you choose to serve will be your master. Do you know that God told Moses to go say to Pharaoh, "Let My people go, that they may serve Me?" Let My people go, that they may serve Me. You have a choice now. Which kingdom do you want to serve—sin that leads to death or righteousness that leads to life?

We get to choose now. There are two kingdoms, and a choice must be made. You can be redeemed from sin and choose to serve righteousness, or you can continue in sin and deceive yourself, thinking you are part of a righteous kingdom while your life shows no fruit or evidence of that kingdom. Or, you can repent of your sin. That's the way of the Kingdom—it's a life of repentance. It's to say, "No, death is not mine and sin is not mine. Holiness and righteousness—that's mine. I serve a holy King."

"Therefore, when He came into the world, He said: 'Sacrifice and offering You did not desire, but a body You have prepared for Me. In burnt offerings and sacrifices for sin, You had no pleasure.' Then I said, 'Behold, I have come—in the volume of the book it is written of Me—to do Your will, O God.'" Hebrews 10:5-7 NKJV

This is Jesus speaking. The sacrifice of bulls and goats didn't please God, but He gave Him something that would please Him—His own body, Jesus Christ Himself becoming the sacrifice.

"Previously saying, 'Sacrifice and offering, burnt offerings, and offerings for sin You did not desire, nor had pleasure in them' (which are offered according to the Law), then He said, 'Behold, I have come to do Your will, O God.' He takes away the first that He may establish the second. By that will we have been sanctified through the offering of the body of Jesus Christ once for all." Hebrews 10:8-9 NKJV

When He says "to do Your will," He is talking about the will of offering His body.

"And every priest stands ministering daily and offering repeatedly the same sacrifices, which can never take away sins. But this Man, after He had offered one sacrifice for sins forever, sat down at the right hand of God, from that time waiting till His enemies are made His footstool. For by one offering He has perfected forever those who are being sanctified. But the Holy Spirit also witnesses to us; for after He had said before, 'This is the covenant that I will make with them after those days, says the Lord: I will put My laws into their hearts, and in their minds I will write them,' then He adds, 'Their sins and their lawless deeds I will remember no more.' Now, where there is remission of these, there is no longer an offering for sin. Therefore, brethren, having boldness to enter the Holiest by the blood of Jesus, by a new and living way which He consecrated for us, through the veil, that is, His flesh, and having a High Priest over the house of God, let us draw near with a true heart in full assurance of faith, having our hearts sprinkled from an evil conscience and our bodies washed with pure water. Let us hold fast the confession of our hope without wavering, for He who promised is faithful." Hebrews 10:11-23 NKJV

Here's what's happening: Jesus made a way for His blood to

wash away our sins. The body of Jesus is the temple—it's the temple. Jesus said, "Tear this temple down, and in three days I'll raise it back up"(John 2:19). He says that we get to pass through the veil, which is His flesh, washed by His blood, and enter into the holy place.

If God is holy, we can't enter that place. Our hands are unclean, but His hands were pierced, and His blood came out so that ours may be cleaned. Do you know that Jesus poured out His blood in seven places—seven times? How many times does the priest have to take the blood and sprinkle it? Seven times. Jesus poured out His blood seven times as the atonement—all over Jerusalem.

His body is the temple, He is the priest, and He is the lamb. His flesh is the veil. His body was torn so the veil could be torn, allowing us to enter in. His blood was poured out to atone for your sins so that you could enter in with Him. He is the priest making the sacrifice, He is the lamb who is the sacrifice, He is the veil that is being torn, and He is the mercy seat that the blood is being poured out on.

He fulfilled what needed to be fulfilled in Himself so that you could become His prize. What kind of King is this? A King whose throne is a cross and whose crown is one of thorns. Why? Because the curse upon man was that he would labor and toil by the sweat of his brow—and Jesus sweat blood to atone and break that curse. The earth would produce thorns, and He would take them as a crown to break that curse off of us as well.

What a King this is—a King who would take a crown of thorns to give us a crown. You know He's going to give you a crown? What kind of King is this? This is a King unlike the rulers of this world who lord it over men. No, He became a servant. He's modeling for us what this kingdom looks like—a kingdom of service. He freed us from the bondage of Egypt so we could serve Him. He freed us from the terror of darkness, from the hand of the wicked, and from death itself so that we may serve and reign over this earth with goodness, not wickedness—not evil.

He died. He took the evil upon Himself so He could give us life, joy, and peace in the Holy Spirit. This is our God—one who made His throne a cross, who made His crown a crown of thorns, and who took our mockery upon Himself. It's by the blood of Jesus that we are sanctified, and it's by His flesh that we are healed. Through His flesh, we can go into the veil, into the holy place, allowing His blood to wash us clean.

Discussion Questions

1. How does recognizing Jesus as both King and Redeemer influence your understanding of His sacrifice on the cross? In what ways does this understanding impact your personal relationship with Him and your daily life?

2. What are some areas in your life or in the world where you see the influence of the Kingdom of Darkness? How can embracing the victory of Jesus over darkness empower you to address these areas?

3. The chapter mentions the choice between serving sin leading to death or obedience leading to righteousness. What practical steps can you take to consistently choose to serve the Kingdom of God? How can you embody being "zealous for good works" in your community and spheres of influence?

7

THE LIFE OF THE KINGDOM

"Now on the first day of the week, very early in the morning, they, and certain other women with them, came to the tomb bringing the spices which they had prepared. But they found the stone rolled away from the tomb. Then they went in and did not find the body of the Lord Jesus. And it happened, as they were greatly perplexed about this, that behold, two men stood by them in shining garments. Then, as they were afraid and bowed their faces to the earth, they said to them, 'Why do you seek the living among the dead? He is not here but is risen! Remember how He spoke to you when He was still in Galilee, saying, "The Son of Man must be delivered into the hands of sinful men, and be crucified, and the third day rise again."' Luke 24:1-7 NKJV

They were looking for the dead. The question was, why are you looking for the living among the dead? But, they were looking for the dead among the dead—they didn't understand it. They missed who Jesus was and I think some of us have missed who Jesus really is. Many people may say, "I'm a believer, I believe in Jesus," but maybe they miss who Jesus really is.

The disciples spent three years walking with Jesus, eating with

Him, watching Him do unthinkable things, and yet they're at a tomb looking for the living among the dead. They missed it. I don't want to miss it, and I don't want you to miss it. I want us to see who Jesus really is today.

In the beginning, God created a good world. He said it was good, and He doesn't lie—He doesn't know how to lie. He is truth and the truth. He said it was good, and in the good world, after making the earth, the seas, the heavens, the birds that fly, and the creatures that crawl, He fashioned a different creation, something that would bring pleasure to Him in a different way than the rest of creation. From the dust of the ground, He created man. He formed man in His likeness and breathed into His nostrils the breath of life. God fellowshipped with man. But, man separated themselves from God. In rebellion, they sinned. The Bible says the wages of sin is death, and all men sinned, so all die. God decided to make His own plan to redeem humanity, to bring us back into a relationship with Himself. He said a seed would come to crush the head of the one who deceived them to rebel in sin and ultimately cause death. Hope for humanity arises that someone would come and deliver them from their enemy. God made a covenant with Abraham, saying, "Abraham, I'm going to bless you, and all nations will be blessed through you."

Then comes David. David is anointed king over the descendants of Abraham. He is from the line of Judah. God says to David, "When you rest with your ancestors, I am going to bring about the one, and He will sit on your throne forever. His kingdom will never end. I will call Him "My Son." Hope begins to rise in Israel for a deliverer—a Savior, a King who would sit on David's throne. When we open the New Testament, Could it be that the King has come—the Savior, the Anointed One who would rule forever and deliver us from our enemy?

Jesus began to say, "Before Abraham, I am." Could it be that

God had come in this man, to deliver us from our enemy, to reign in a kingdom forever? He announced, "The Kingdom of God is at hand," He healed the sick and delivered the captives, just as He said He would 600 years before through the prophet Isaiah. He drew crowds of people whose hopes began to rise and rise and rise. The Savior is here. We know Him. His name is Jesus, and they followed Him.

Jesus said, "Who do they say I am?" Peter's response was, "Oh, some say this, but we know You are the Son of God, the Savior of the world. We know it." He said, "The Father has shown you this. No man has revealed this to you. God has shown you this."

Then, on one confusing night, Jesus is betrayed by His own followers. He is nailed to a criminal's cross, charged with things that He never did. But in the verdict, Pilate said, "He's innocent: I'm going to let Him go." But, the Israelites—the very people He came for, the descendants of Abraham—said, "No, crucify Him! Kill Him. We don't want Him. Let His blood be upon our hands." And they whipped Him and nailed Him to a cross and crucified Him.

Above the cross, it said, "The King of the Jews." This King didn't become King the way kings of the world become kings—with power and force—but instead with sacrifice. Instead of a golden throne, He had a wooden one. Instead of fighting His enemy with iron, He fought Him with wood—a cross. He was enthroned upon the cross. When He breathed His last and said, "It is finished," all His disciples were confused, saying to themselves, "I thought this was the King? I thought this was our Savior? I thought He would reign forever?" And all their hopes were crushed.

So, as these women came to the tomb, they weren't coming because they were expecting a resurrection. No, they were coming to say goodbye to their friend, to their hopes. They were coming to honor, for one last time, maybe a prophet. Because they were confused. They didn't understand. They missed it. They had missed who He was. "Why are you looking for the living among the dead? He's not here."

You see, I want to declare that Jesus has always been among the living. Before the resurrection, He was among the living. Before Abraham, He was among the living. Before He was born in a manger, this One, Jesus, was among the living. In fact, we were the ones who weren't among the living. But Jesus, the Living One, came to bring us into the land of the living—to be among the living.

> *"And the Lord God formed man of the dust of the ground, and breathed into his nostrils the breath of life; and man became a living being." Genesis 2:7 NKJV*

God actually made you and me to be living beings. When we rebelled against God and took from the Tree, it was as if the breath of life was knocked out of us. We walked, but not among the living. We were the walking dead. But the Living One planned to bring us back into fellowship with the living. So, the Living One came and was born as a man. He walked among the dead. John chapter one says;

> *"In the beginning the Word already existed. The Word was with God, and the Word was God. He existed in the beginning with God. God created everything through him, and nothing was created except through him.*
> *The Word gave life to everything that was created, and his life brought light to everyone. The light shines in the darkness, and the darkness can never extinguish it. God sent a man, John the Baptist, to tell about the light so that everyone might believe because of his testimony. John himself was not the light; he was*

simply a witness to tell about the light. The one who is the true light, who gives light to everyone, was coming into the world.
He came into the very world he created, but the world didn't recognize him. He came to his own people, and even they rejected him. But to all who believed him and accepted him, he gave the right to become children of God. They are reborn—not with a physical birth resulting from human passion or plan, but a birth that comes from God.
So the Word became human and made his home among us. He was full of unfailing love and faithfulness. And we have seen his glory, the glory of the Father's one and only Son.
John testified about him when he shouted to the crowds, "This is the one I was talking about when I said, 'Someone is coming after me who is far greater than I am, for he existed long before me.'" From his abundance we have all received one gracious blessing after another. For the law was given through Moses, but God's unfailing love and faithfulness came through Jesus Christ. No one has ever seen God. But the unique One, who is himself God, is near to the Father's heart. He has revealed God to us.." John 1:1-18 NLT

In the beginning, God. He was life. He created everything, and everything that had life had life because of Him. We rejected this life, and the result was death. But, this life fashioned a plan to bring life back to us. We missed it. We didn't see it. Some saw it and rejected it. But the disciples—they saw, and they walked with the living One, who walked with life among the dead. There was One who walked with life. There is this testimony of John in 1 John chapter one;

"That which was from the beginning, which we have heard, which we have seen with our eyes, which we have looked upon, and our hands have handled, concerning the Word of life—the life was manifested, and we have seen, and bear witness, and declare to you that eternal life which was with the Father and was manifested to us—that which we have seen and heard we declare to you, that you

also may have fellowship with us; and truly our fellowship is with the Father and with His Son Jesus Christ. And these things we write to you that your joy may be full." 1 John 1:1-4 NKJV

He says, "We testify that we saw the Living One. He walked among us. We touched Him. We handled Him. He was life. He was from the Father, but He manifested life to us. We testify to you so you'll believe and that your joy will be full."

"See, I have set before you today life and good, death and evil, in that I command you today to love the Lord your God, to walk in His ways, and to keep His commandments, His statutes, and His judgments, that you may live and multiply; and the Lord your God will bless you in the land which you go to possess." Deuteronomy 30:15-16 NKJV

"I call heaven and earth as witnesses today against you, that I have set before you life and death, blessing and cursing; therefore choose life, that both you and your descendants may live; that you may love the Lord your God, that you may obey His voice, and that you may cling to Him, for He is your life and the length of your days; and that you may dwell in the land which the Lord swore to your fathers, to Abraham, Isaac, and Jacob, to give them." Deuteronomy 30:19-20 NKJV

He says, "I present before you today life and death. Choose life." We're discovering that life has a name. His name is Jesus. There's only One who is living. He says, "I present Him before you because your God will be life to you." Jesus said in John 11:

"I am the resurrection and the life. He who believes in Me, though he dies, he shall live, and whoever lives and believes in Me shall never die." John 11:25-26 NKJV

"I am the way, the truth, and the life. No one comes to the Father except through Me." John 14:6 NKJV

"And this is eternal life, that they may know You, the only true God, and Jesus Christ whom You have sent." John 17:3 NKJV

This is life, that you would know God who is life.

"For God so loved the world that He gave His only begotten Son, that whoever believes in Him should not perish but have everlasting life." John 3:16 NKJV

God loved the world so much that He sent life, so that whoever would believe in Him would receive life. He didn't send His Son into the world to condemn the world, but to give the world life.

You and I were not made to die. That's why when someone passes, sometimes we'll say they passed before their time. But do you know, even if you die at 130, you've passed before your time? Because you were never meant to die. That's why people will say, "Well, if God is good, then how come we had a pandemic? How come this and that? If God is good, then how come so much death?" We get it twisted. We chose death when we rejected life. So how come there's so much death? Because so many have rejected life.

And even when we chose death, Life still put on flesh and came to us so that we may have life and have it abundantly. The enemy comes to steal, kill, and destroy, but I have come that you may have life and have it abundantly. Life has a name, and His name is Jesus. So, how come death spit Him out? Because death can never extinguish life. Never. He who has no beginning and no end allowed Himself to have an end so that you may know life is more powerful than death. The One who could have no end allowed Himself to have an end so that we would know that life is more powerful than death. Choose life.

In the beginning, God formed man from the dust of the earth, and He breathed into his nostrils the breath of life. Jesus left the tomb and found His disciples in John chapter 20, verse 22, He breathed on them and said, "Receive My Spirit." He is saying receive life again! He's inviting them and you and me to walk among the living with His life. The same Spirit, the same breath that raised Christ from the dead, now is giving you new life. Peter, after encountering the man at the gate called Beautiful, said:

"Silver and gold I do not have, but what I do have I give you: In the name of Jesus Christ of Nazareth, rise up and walk." Acts 3:6 NKJV

And the man walked, because being crippled has to do with death—that doesn't have to do with life. But Peter had received life, and life was bursting through him, giving life to others. So, the man got up and walked, and the masses began to look at them. They said, "Why do you look at us as if we did this, as if we were able to do this for this man? No, Jesus did this." Peter continued:

"But you denied the Holy One and the Just, and asked for a murderer to be granted to you, and killed the Prince of life, whom God raised from the dead, of which we are witnesses." Acts 3:14-15 NKJV

In Acts chapter 2, Peter said:

"But God raised Him up again, putting an end to the agony of death, since it was impossible for Him to be held in its power." Acts 2:24 NASB1995

Death tried to take hold of Life and got burned. It had to let

Him up. Our God is a consuming fire. Death tried to take hold of Life and couldn't keep its grip on Him. Death had to let Him up. The Bible says that when you believe, Life itself—Jesus Christ—comes to live inside of you. And that one day, death will try to take hold of you, but it will have to give you up because Life lives in you, and death cannot conquer life.

"And this is the testimony: that God has given us eternal life, and this life is in His Son. He who has the Son has life; he who does not have the Son of God does not have life. These things I have written to you who believe in the name of the Son of God, that you may know that you have eternal life, and that you may continue to believe in the name of the Son of God." 1 John 5:11-13 NKJV

The scriptures repeatedly tell us that they testify to us: eternal life is found in Jesus Christ because He is life. Today, I set before you life and death. I recommend that you choose life. Some of us have been walking with Jesus for many years, and we celebrate—we have to celebrate—because we knew what death was. We walked in it every day. Then, when we met Jesus, something happened to us. I know because it happened to me.

I was nine years old, riding my bike the day before Easter. I saw some people having an egg hunt. In my house, egg hunts were done with hard-boiled eggs. But this house had eggs with candy inside. I thought to myself, "What?" Apparently, my parents didn't know! I sat there on my bike and watched them gather these eggs. When they opened them, Starbursts, Snickers and all kinds of wonderful things fell out instead of an egg yolk.

This family looked at me, watching from my bike, and they said, "Do you want to come and join us?" I threw my bike down, started pushing kids, and took their eggs! They invited me to come and sit down, and they began to tell me about this man named Jesus. And something in my soul was hearing something—

something I knew, but didn't fully understand—something that I knew was for me. And I said 'Yes' to Him.

When they asked, "Do you want to receive Jesus as Lord and give your life to Him?" I said, "Yes, I do." And life came inside me. At nine years old, something changed inside me. I had passed from death to life.

But, my family didn't go to church. Slowly but surely, I continued walking on the path—some days on the path of life, saying, "Lord, forgive me", and some days on the path of death. By 19, I was completely walking on the path of death again. I was calling out to God, and I got invited to church. I went to church, bowed my head, and said, "Jesus". I just whispered His name. And He came. He showed up and brought life. And all the darkness that was filling my heart fled at the light.

Then joy, love, and peace filled my heart. I've never left this life. In that moment, I took hold of life and said, "You're not getting away this time." But He said, "No, no, you're not getting away this time. Follow Me." And I began to follow Jesus Christ, the Person of Life. I've felt life ever since. And when I die, it will not be the end of me—just a comma in my story—because I walk among the living. Death can't hold me because life lives inside of me.

Today, that same Person I met—Jesus Christ—wants to be in every life around the world. Life is calling our name. He laid His life down so that we could have it. He took death to give us life. I believe all of us want life. Choose life.

Discussion Questions

1. How does viewing Jesus as the embodiment of life change your perception of His role in your personal faith? In what ways can recognizing Jesus as the "Living One" impact how you live your daily life?

2. This chapter presents the choice between life and death as a central theme. What are some practical ways you can choose life in your decisions and actions? Have there been times when you, like the disciples, struggled to understand or recognize Jesus' presence in your life? How did you overcome that?

3. How does the concept of eternal life influence your priorities and goals? In light of the invitation to all to recieve Jesus, how might you share this message of life with others?

8

HE IS RISEN

"But on the first day of the week, at early dawn, they came to the tomb bringing the spices which they had prepared. And they found the stone rolled away from the tomb, but when they entered, they did not find the body of the Lord Jesus. While they were perplexed about this, behold, two men suddenly stood near them in dazzling clothing; and as the women were terrified and bowed their faces to the ground, the men said to them, "Why do you seek the living One among the dead? He is not here, but He has risen. Remember how He spoke to you while He was still in Galilee, saying that the Son of Man must be delivered into the hands of sinful men, and be crucified, and the third day rise again." And they remembered His words, and returned from the tomb and reported all these things to the eleven and to all the rest." Luke 24:1-9 NASB1995

The statement the angels make, "He is not here, but He has risen," is the foundation of Christianity. If there is no resurrection, we have no faith, we have no hope. A dead savior is no savior; there has to be a resurrection. When we remember the resurrection, we must understand the power of the resurrection. It is not just power for the future; there is a revelation in it for us today that causes us to live differently in resurrection power every single day of our lives. I pray we get a deeper revelation of what the power of the resurrection means for us today. We have been given something in the resurrection that changes our every day, not just for when we die. Every day we are to walk in resurrection power.

"Jesus answered them, "To you it has been granted to know the mysteries of the kingdom of heaven, but to them it has not been granted.'" Matthew 13:11 NASB1995

The "to them" is referring to those who do not know Him. There are mysteries hidden in the scriptures. There are mysteries in the Kingdom, and I want you to know the mysteries of the power of the resurrection. There is a mystery in it.

"The mystery of which was hidden for ages and generations [from angels and men], but is now revealed to His holy people (the saints), To whom God was pleased to make known how great for the Gentiles are the riches of the glory of this mystery, which is Christ within and among you, the Hope of [realizing the] glory." Colossians 1:26-27 AMPC

This mystery of Christ living in you, the resurrected King of Kings living inside of you, is a mystery. There are mysteries even within that mystery that I want you to know so you can walk in the fullness of what God intended you to walk in.

"Blessed be the God and Father of our Lord Jesus Christ, who according to His abundant mercy has begotten us again to a living hope through the resurrection of Jesus Christ from the dead." 1 Peter 1:3 NKJV

In the Greek, the word "begotten" actually means to be born again. The phrase "living hope" is actually "hope living"; the word "hope" is first and means "an expectation". The word "living" in Greek is "zoe", which is abundant life. So we have an expectation of abundant life because of the mercy of the Father. We now have an expectation of abundant life because of the resurrection. I want you to live the abundant life, to live every day with the expectation that abundant life is yours and it should pour out from you. Jesus said in John 10:10, "that you may have life and life more abundantly." It is the same word for living in 1 Peter 1:3; it is the "zoe" life, the God life. This is the good life; this is the life Jesus had even before the cross. He had "zoe," He had abundant life—that is why death had to spit Him up. You now have that life living inside of you, and you have the expectation of it in the future. But I want you to see, if you do not walk in the "zoe" now, you will not have the "zoe" then. The mystery of the abundant life is supposed to be a revelation you walk in every single day; it is supposed to be a manifestation you walk in every day. If it is, He says you can be assured that you will rise. Jesus already had abundant life, and death could not conquer it. The Bible says it now lives inside of you; the same Spirit that raised Christ from the dead now lives in you, giving you new life. We have been born again by the Spirit that raised Christ from the dead; now we have an expectation of "zoe" living inside of us because of the resurrection of Jesus.

> *"...through the resurrection of Jesus Christ from the dead, to an inheritance incorruptible and undefiled and that does not fade away, reserved in heaven for you, who are kept by the power of God through faith for salvation ready to be revealed in the last time." 1 Peter 1:3-5 NKJV*

Now when we look at these words in Greek, what he is trying to say is you cannot lose it; it does not get old, and it is not like bread that molds. This life is not like silver or gold; it will not tarnish. This life is actually supposed to be as good as the day you believed—from glory to glory it should abound for you and from you. It is an inheritance that you received because of what Jesus did. It is reserved; the word "reserved" means protected. It is the power of God that is protects both you and it. He is saying it is kept and held for you, and it is faith that brings you into it. We do not live by sight; we do not walk by that; we do not live according to what we see around us, but it is faith that leads us. He is saying it is your faith that will bring you into the fullness of that which will be revealed. There is even more—from glory to glory—until one day we enter the fullness of it. This revelation of the resurrection of Jesus is supposed to do something. The world does not have what you have; they do not have that which makes us a peculiar people.

The death and resurrection of Jesus mean a few things for us:

- **Demonstration of the Love of God**: It is the demonstration of the love of God and how He feels about you. He loves you; there is no love that has ever been expressed like the love expressed in the death and resurrection of Jesus Christ. We need to know He did not have to die for us; He chose to die for us.
The cross is an eternal declaration, a statement of His love for you.
- **An Exchange**: Something was needed, and that is why He had to come. It was an exchange of the only begotten for those who would become sons and daughters. On the cross, He was the only begotten of God at that moment, but now because of that, millions have become begotten of God, and millions more will come into the Kingdom.
- **Expression of Grace**: The resurrection is an expression of God's grace to bring man back into His glorious position and state; it was His grace to do this.
- **Proof of Power Over Death**: The resurrection proves that death no longer has the right or the power to reign over mankind, over your

life. Death has been reigning over humanity. But now, because of the death and resurrection of Christ, we have proof that death no longer has the right to reign over your life. We need to understand this to understand the mystery of the resurrection of Jesus Christ. The resurrection is a triumph over death, but we must understand death and its power to understand the greater power of the resurrection.

The Power of Death

1. **Death is the greatest fear of all humanity**: It is the thing all men have to face. It is the fear of all; for those outside of Christ, it is the period at the end of life that is awaiting everyone.
2. **Every religion makes it its point to answer the question of death.**
3. **Death is the only power that has control over every human:** Anxiety has power over some, depression has power over some, but death has had power over all.
4. **No one can resist death:** even Jesus had to pass through it.
5. **No one can avoid it**: This is the power of death before the resurrection—it reigned over all. Death is a big bully demonstrating its authority and power and reign over every human until Jesus. *"And as it is appointed for men to die once, but after this the judgment." Hebrews 9:27 NKJV*
6. **Death is an equalizer:** You could be the queen of England, but you are going to be buried in the ground. You might be the beggar on the street; you could be in the palace, but at some point, we will both find the same thing. Death is an equalizer.

In the parable of the rich man and Lazarus (see Luke 16:19-31), Lazarus was a beggar, and the rich man did not help the beggar. The parable goes on to say that the rich man finds himself dead just like the poor man. But when the rich man looks, he sees that the man who was once the beggar is now free. He is free from his poverty; he is now with Abraham, and every one of his needs is met. The rich man now has nothing but torment, and he longs for the poor beggar to dip his finger in water and put it on his tongue. Death is an equalizer.

I want us to understand the resurrection and its power, but to do so, we must ask the question: why does death exist? Where did it come from? Who created it? Death has always existed; even in the beginning, death was always there.

"And the Lord God commanded the man, saying, 'Of every tree of the garden you may freely eat; but of the tree of the knowledge of good and evil you shall not eat, for in the day that you eat of it you shall surely die.'" Genesis 2:16-17 NKJV

Death was there in the garden; life was there, and death was there. But death had no power. It was dormant. The one reigning was life; life was reigning over everything. Life had the power. Death was there in isolation without power. So, what gave death its power? Because Jesus came to conquer death, but why was death reigning? What gave it its power to reign? The scripture says if you eat from this tree, you will surely die. Meaning if you do this(eat), then you will activate this(death). You will give power to something. And what was that thing? It was sin; it was the disobedience. Do not do this. And if you do, you will activate the reign of this. Sin is what gives death its power. The power of death is sin. The reason death has been able to reign over humanity is because of sin. So God does not come and just conquer death; He first has to conquer sin. This is why we need the cross. Death has reigned because all have sinned. The sinless one comes, is born, and walks the earth. He wants to die in your place so that you may have the "zoe" life He has—the everlasting abundant life. He said, "I came that you may have 'zoe' life abundantly—the eternal life. Jesus was saying, "that is what I want you to have; that is what I have, and I want to give it to you."

But to do that, He does not just have to die; He has to pay for sin. He has to conquer sin, and if He conquers sin, He takes the power away from death—that is what He came to do. To take the power away from death. But Jesus was not a candidate for death. That is a problem; the only thing that will activate death is sin, but Jesus had no sin. He was not a candidate for death. The Living One walked the earth without sinning; He was not a candidate to die. Death had no power over Him. The ruler of death, Satan, had no power over Him. Jesus said, "The ruler of this world is coming, but he has nothing in Me." He was not afraid of him because death had no power, no right to His life. So what is He to do? Jesus wants to die to give us life, but He is not a candidate for death. So on the cross, God, who is eternal, who is in the future and the past, takes your sin and everyone who will ever believe and places it on Him. The only way He can die is if your sins are on Him. He is not a candidate for death otherwise. This is how someone who stands outside of time is able to go into the future to those who will put their faith in Him and say, "Okay, I will take your sin and put it on Him."

The only reason Jesus was able to die was because your sin was upon Him. So when you believe in Jesus, your sins are removed, and you are declared righteous. The proof was that Jesus was able to die. He could not die because He had no sin; sin had to be placed on Him. The proof of your righteousness is the death of Jesus Christ, because He could not die if your sin remained on you and not on Him. He would have stayed living—there was a great exchange. His righteousness was given to you, and your sin was put on Him. I want you to live with a revelation of your righteousness—your freedom from the power of sin and death. So, if the sin has been removed and you are declared righteous, death has no power over you. This is why Jesus says, "I am the resurrection and the life; anyone who believes in Me lives, even if he dies." Death has lost its sting; its power has been lost from you and from me. This is the good news of the resurrection.

"Inasmuch then as the children have partaken of flesh and blood, He Himself likewise shared in the same, that through death He might destroy him who had the power of death, that is, the devil, and release those who through fear of death were all their lifetime subject to bondage." Hebrews 2:14-15 NKJV

He became like us, then died in our place so that the one who had the power of death—Satan, the devil—would lose it, and those who were bound by the fear of it all their lives would be free. You should be free from the power of the fear of death.

"So when this corruptible has put on incorruption, and this mortal has put on immortality, then shall be brought to pass the saying that is written: 'Death is swallowed up in victory.' 'O Death, where is your sting? O Hades, where is your victory?'" 1 Corinthians 15:54-55 NKJV

Think of a bee. If it has no ability to sting you, it might as well be a housefly. When we see a bee, we are like, "Oh hey, whoa," and certain bees have certain stings that make us think, "Do not mess with that bee." But a housefly? We are like, "Okay, whatever, get away from me." You are not freaking out, saying, "Oh gosh, it is a housefly." You just think, "Yeah, whatever, it's just a fly. I do not necessarily want it in my house; it is an irritant." But it has nothing to produce fear in you. That is what has happened to death. Paul was mocking death. He had a revelation of the life in Christ through the resurrection, and he mocked it. "Where is your sting? Where is your victory?"

Even when beloved saints die, they live. They enter the fullness of the revelation of Christ, of the living. All of the pain is gone. We mourn because we lose loved ones and friends, but they are living. If there were no death and resurrection, it would be very hard, but because of the death and resurrection, they are among the living. The Bible says we are surrounded by witnesses—a living cloud of witnesses. First, the scripture talks about how they died; they all died. But now we are surrounded by them because they are not dead. Though they die, they live. And He says you are being watched by every single person who went before you and proclaimed the faith that you have today. He says they are watching you. Run! Strip off that which entangles you, which is sin, which gives death its power. Strip it off and run the race. Put your eyes on Jesus.

I do not live with the fear of death. I do not want you to live with the fear of death. I am not afraid to die in my 30s, 40s, 50s—I do not care. Because I am among the living, and death has no power over me. We need to get this. If I were to pass, some may miss me, some may not. Some may be glad I am gone. But since the moment I believed, death has lost. Death does not get to celebrate when I die. It has lost its power. It knows, "Yeah, him too, he will rise." All the past and all the future of those who believe and put their trust in the Lord will rise. Do you know that when Jesus died, tombs were opened? Those who had believed in the Lord even before the cross came walking out. Can you imagine what that was like? I can see it: "Is that David? Is that Nehemiah? Is that Jeremiah? What are you doing here?" They say, "Oh, death has lost its grip upon me." This happened. It is recorded by historians, not just believers.

This is why with Christianity, people have tried so hard to

prove it false and they cannot. And when they talk about it or research it, it proves itself more true. Every person that has researched it to prove it untrue has found that it was true. Then they think, "Let us just not talk about it, because the more we try to debunk it, the more we realize it is true." And the more the truth is revealed, the more power truth is given. Historians, people who were not believers, wrote about these events. The death and resurrection of Jesus Christ is recorded by historians. Imagine someone who did what Jesus did. He got the attention of historians. Their whole job is like reporters—to let the known world know what is happening in different places. Well, someone is walking on water and feeding crowds too large to count with a boy's lunch. He is healing; the blind see, the mute speak, the lame walk. And they are recording it. And it comes to a moment when this amazing man is being murdered—falsely accused and murdered. They were recording this, and it is like the sad emoji moment.

But then, on the third day, He rose again. They had to write this story down. I am telling you, historians recorded it, not just the apostles. This is what they found. People try to prove it to be fiction, but when they study it, they see, "No, no, no, it is not just the disciples recording this. Historians everywhere were following and recording." So, there is no point for them to lie. And the only way we know something is true—the only way we know Alexander the Great lived—is because of history, paintings, clay pots, and historical writings. If we do not have them, then he did not exist. We have to have a certain amount of things to prove someone actually lived in the past, and Jesus is the most recorded person in history—not just His life, but also His death, burial, and resurrection. He walked the earth for forty days after His resurrection. It says at one moment five hundred people gathered around and listened to Him. They watched Him die, watched Him be buried, three days dead, watched Him come back from the dead and walk among them still with holes in His hands and feet, yet now living. For forty days—just over a month—He was just hanging out. And at one moment, 500 gathered around Him to listen to Him teach after the resurrection. There was not a "maybe I saw him" moment. It was not a "kind of" experience. They ate with Him and everything, and then He did like Neo from The Matrix—straight up into Heaven, and they watched it.

If it was made up, it would just be forgotten. Even the high priest and Sanhedrin were all part of witnessing this and the cover-up. It speaks about how they tried to cover it up in the scriptures. They paid the guards who were there when the angels showed up and then Mary and the others showed up. When the angel showed up, it says the guards saw, they trembled and fell over as if dead. They saw the angel; they saw the tombstone roll away. At first, they thought it was an earthquake, but then, boom, an angel shows up. And at every point in scripture when an angel shows up, the fear of God is put into the atmosphere. And these Roman soldiers, these hardened men who have killed men, fall over. They faint. And the angel says, "Hey, hey, I know you are here about Jesus. Do not be afraid. I have to tell you something. Why are you looking for the living among the dead? He is not here. Remember what He told you, that the Son of Man would die at the hands of men, but on the third day He would rise again." And they remembered what He said. But what He said was too impossible to believe until they saw it with their own eyes. Even the apostles and disciples, when they came and were told what happened said, "No, it cannot be." I love how when Jesus healed the blind man, he said, "Has anyone ever done this?" Imagine what they had to think after Jesus died and was raised from the dead. No one was praying for Him to rise from the dead; they did not believe. They watched His body be mutilated. They must have thought, "There is no way that can be restored." But thankfully, life—the Spirit of life—came. I want us to walk in the same power of life.

"And if Christ is not risen, your faith is futile; you are still in your sins! Then also those who have fallen asleep in Christ have perished. If in this life only we have hope in Christ, we are of all men the most pitiable." 1 Corinthians 15:17-19 NKJV

If there is no resurrection, if there is no conquering of the power of death, then sin still has its power over you and your faith is futile. Paul thinks death is just falling asleep. They no longer view the death of saints as death but simply as falling asleep. But, if Christ has not been raised from the dead, then they have not fallen asleep—they have perished. Sin still has its power, meaning death still has its power, which means those who have fallen asleep are not asleep; they are dead.

"But now Christ is risen from the dead, and has become the firstfruits of those who have fallen asleep. For since by man came death, by Man also came the resurrection of the dead. For as in Adam all die, even so in Christ all shall be made alive." 1 Corinthians 15:20-22 NKJV

Paul is trying to make sure we understand this: without the death and resurrection, sin has not lost its power, death has not lost its power, and we have no hope. But that is not the case. Thanks be to God who raised Christ from the dead.

"There is therefore now no condemnation to those who are in Christ Jesus, who do not walk according to the flesh, but according to the Spirit. For the law of the Spirit of life in Christ Jesus has made me free from the law of sin and death." Romans 8:1-2 NKJV

Now I want to look at some of the mysteries so we can walk in the power of the resurrection. We need to understand there are three heavens revealed in the scriptures(2 Corinthians 12:2). The first heaven is where the birds and planes fly. The second heaven is where powers, thrones, and dominions—demonic powers—rule. But in the third heaven, there is a King. Who is that King? Jesus. And His Kingdom is to reign over all thrones, all powers, and all dominions. We have been seated with Him in the third heaven to reign over every principality, power, throne, and dominion.

Where does death have its power? In the second heaven. But the law of the Spirit of life in Christ reigns over the third heaven, and the law of sin and death reigns over the second heaven. The law of the Spirit of life in Christ is the gospel. The law of sin and death is the Old Testament Mosaic law. So, when you transgress the second heaven, what does it give power to? Sin and death; you activate the law of sin and death. But when you, according to 1 John 1:9, confess your sins, He is faithful and just to forgive you and cleanse you of all unrighteousness. And if you have no unrighteousness, you are righteous. Every door in the second heaven must be shut to you. Sin, death, and evil are not to have power over your life. That does not mean we cannot give it power, but it does not have to.

Paul makes it clear this is for those who do not walk according to the flesh but according to the Spirit. If we walk according to the flesh and gratify the flesh, then we will open the power of sin and death to our lives. The resurrection is the conquering of sin and death. Because His blood has been shed, He has taken the power of death, shut the second heaven to you and me and declared us righteous to come boldly before the throne of grace and sit with Him in the third heaven.

"For what the law could not do in that it was weak through the flesh, God did by sending His own Son in the likeness of sinful flesh, on account of sin: He condemned sin in the flesh, that the righteous requirement of the law might be fulfilled in us who do not walk according to the flesh but according to the Spirit. For those who live according to the flesh set their minds on the things of the flesh, but

those who live according to the Spirit, the things of the Spirit. For to be carnally minded is death, but to be spiritually minded is life and peace." Romans 8:3-6 NKJV

He is referring to the Mosaic law. I do not want you to activate death through sin and be like Adam and Eve, who continue to activate the power of death in your life. Sickness and anxiety, fear itself, is evidence of the activation of the second heaven in your life—of the power of death. But it's a wonderful gift because I always say Satan is like a bad card player; he always overplays his hand. If I am sick, I know I have done something—I have opened up the second heaven.

I love this example of Elisha: he is being too much of a spiritual father, he is raising too many spiritual sons, and he has too many in the school of the prophets and needs to make a bigger space. Someone borrowed an axe head to do so, and when he was cutting down some trees, the axe head flew into the river. The man gasped, screamed out because it was borrowed. It was very expensive; he could not pay for it. He was going to be in trouble. So Elisha says, "Show me where it fell." Show me where you lost it. So, when I have something going on in my life that is the evidence of the power of the second heaven trying to show its dominion over my life. I just go back to where it started. Where did I lose my peace? Where did I lose the healing? Where did I begin to see this come in? And I pray, "Holy One, can you show me? Have I given the second heaven any right in my life?" And He will say something like, "Yeah, in this area, when you talked to your son, or your wife, or this person in this way."

Peter says your prayers can be hindered by the way you treat your wife. If I have something, I go, "Okay, it is as simple as repentance because I have the antidote for sin available to me—it is the blood of Jesus, and I have to walk humbly before God every day and be led by the Spirit so I can live according to the law of the

Spirit of life in Christ." But there is something even better. The Bible says if I do, then the third heaven has full reign. We want the third heaven to reign in your life.

Deuteronomy 28:1-14 is the reign of the third heaven for those who obey. But Deuteronomy 28:15 and on—what does he talk about? The reign of the second heaven. It is the taking away of all and shutting the third heaven; you will be the tail and not the head, sickness, and all these things that visited Egypt will visit you. The evidence of all these things is just the evidence that we have transgressed the law of sin and death. Great, then we repent, shut the door, and obey, and we open a better door. You know the scriptures talk about doors, and John says, "I saw a door open in Heaven." There are doors and windows in the spirit apparently, and they can be open or shut. If there is no blessing pouring out —no joy, no peace, no health or prosperity—these things or the things Deuteronomy 28:1-14 says shall overtake you. It is not a big deal; It just means we shut the third heaven. Now we repent. It takes the nature of Christ. He said "Let that which was in Him be in you. Though He was God, He did not think of equality with God as something, but He humbled Himself and died on the cross, a criminal's death"(Philippians 2). It is humility; you have to be self-aware. Humble enough to evaluate: Have I opened a door? Because the antidote to shut second heaven is too easy. But, you cannot claim to be walking in the "zoe" abundant life and not have Deuteronomy 28:1-14 taking over your life.

The reign of God should take over, and His blessings and favor shall take over. If something else is taking over, it is not supposed to. We have given it power. Let us take its power back through repentance. It does not matter what title you put on my name; I can transgress it as fast as anyone. I promise a lot of people get more grace than I do because I am a leader in the body of Christ. How many of you know kids get more grace than parents? If you were to walk through a grocery store and a parent is acting like a two-year-old, you would not think about that parent the way you would think about that child. We see a child screaming, and we think, "Oh, they are probably tired." But if we see a grown adult in a grocery store screaming out with a temper tantrum over how they want Oreos, we think, "Get up; you are a grown adult." We would not give them the same grace, I promise you. If you saw me do that and my wife was with me, you would think, "Okay, she needs to leave him." You would not give me the grace. But if you see a little kid, you think, "Okay, they are tired or addicted to sugar," but you would give them some grace. As we mature in Christ, we do not get the same grace.

The Lord thinks, "No, you know the law of the Spirit of life in Christ. You have been tested in it, you have passed those tests, and now you are regressing?" See, Satan would love for me to open that door. You know how fast he would come? He is waiting for a door to be opened. If he gets someone that just got saved, he is happy, but if he can take out pastors and leaders, he rejoices. If they open a door, he is coming. If you open a door, we just shut the door. I am not afraid of this; it has lost its power. I have the antidote—it is the blood of Jesus; it is repentance. I am not trying to add fear; I am trying to take it away by causing people to think about how they live so they live according to the Spirit of life in Christ. God cannot help Himself; He is trying to pour out His blessing, but He will not transgress the second heaven. If you open a door, He says, "I gave you an antidote." But the Lord will keep the law; He wants you to triumph over that law with a greater more excellent law. The gospel is a better covenant, and He has given you the antidote to reign over the Mosaic law with the gospel of Jesus Christ, with the law of the Spirit of life in Christ, He has given you the antidote to reign over it.

We have to choose to walk in Zoe, the abundant life, every single day. This is our right. It is our inheritance in Christ. The scripture says faith is the substance of things hoped for. The word substance means "legal document." Faith says we have the right to something. If I have the deed to my house, it's mine: my name is on it—not the bank's name. If you come and say, "This is my house," I will say, "No, it's not." You could say it a thousand times, and I would still say, "No, it's not." You could take me to court, but I will have a legal document that says it belongs to me. Faith is that I have the legal document; the verdict is out—I possess something. Faith is the substance, the legal guarantee of your expectation. The expectation is the promises of God, the Zoe life, the abundant life being yours forever. Faith says you understand that you have a legal document that says all the promises of God, everything that belonged to Adam and Eve that was lost, is now your right. Everything that Jesus purchased on the cross is your right. Faith says, "That's mine." Deuteronomy 28:1-14 is mine because of Christ Jesus, His death reigning over sin and His resurrection reigning over death. It is the evidence that death has no power and sin has no power over you. If we transgress, we just have to repent and say, "No, no, no, Lord, forgive me—that's not the way of life." The door shuts—boom. Rebuke the devil and walk according to the Spirit of life in Christ.

Pray with me: *Heavenly Father thank you for giving me the right to life and freedom from sin and death because of Jesus Christ. We give you thanks Lord! Yours is the victory and the glory forever, Lord. We declare that we have life, peace and freedom. That we shall live and reign with You forever. We declare Your triumph at the empty tomb is our triumph over death. We thank You for the blood of Jesus, and we thank You for the resurrection. In Jesus' name, amen!*

Discussion Questions

1. How does the resurrection of Jesus Christ change your perspective on sin and death in your own life? In what ways can acknowledging victory over death through Jesus influence how you face fears or challenges?

2. What does living in the "abundant life" that Jesus offers look like in practical terms for you? How can you actively walk in the Spirit of life in Christ to experience this abundant life every day?

3. What are some areas in your life where walking according to the flesh has hindered you, and how can you shift to walking according to the Spirit? How does understanding the laws of the Spirit of life versus the law of sin and death affect your daily decisions and actions?

CONCLUSION
LIVING AS CITIZENS OF THE KINGDOM

As we conclude our exploration of Jesus and the Kingdom, we are faced with a powerful invitation: to not only understand the kingdom but to live as its active, empowered citizens. Through the pages of this book, we've seen the profound need for a kingdom, God's promise to establish it, its arrival in the person of Jesus Christ, the way and culture of this kingdom, and Jesus' victory over death to inaugurate God's domain on earth. Now, we are called to respond—not just with our minds, but with our lives.

A Kingdom Not of This World

The Kingdom of God is not merely an abstract theological concept; it is a present reality and a future hope. Jesus brought this kingdom to earth, and through His death, burial, resurrection, and the outpouring of the Holy Spirit, He has empowered us to live as citizens of this Kingdom today. The Kingdom is where God's rule and reign are recognized and manifested in our lives. Jesus Himself declared, "The kingdom of God is within you" (Luke 17:21).

Our journey as kingdom citizens begins by understanding

that we are no longer bound by the systems and powers of this world. The way of the Kingdom is radically different from the world's values. It is a way of service, love, sacrifice, and humility. The culture of this Kingdom is one of grace, mercy, justice, and peace. It is a Kingdom where we live by the Spirit and are called to be agents of transformation in a broken world.

A Kingdom with a Mission

In light of all we've learned, the question we must ask ourselves is: How does this Kingdom shape how we live, work, and interact with the world around us? How do we embody the Kingdom values in our everyday lives?

First, we must embrace the call to be ambassadors of the Kingdom. Just as Jesus demonstrated God's rule on earth, we are now called to demonstrate the Kingdom in all areas of life. Whether in our homes, workplaces, communities, or nations, we are to bring the rule of God into every sphere. This means seeking justice, promoting peace, showing love, and making disciples.

Second, we are called to live in alignment with the Kingdom's way. This is not a life of convenience or comfort, but one that is marked by self-sacrifice and obedience to God's will. We are to follow Jesus' example, living with the mindset of a servant and the heart of a kingdom ambassador. The values of the Kingdom often stand in stark contrast to the world's values, and it is in this difference that we reflect the light of Christ to those around us.

A Kingdom of Hope

Lastly, we must live with the hope of the coming Kingdom in mind. While the Kingdom has been inaugurated in Christ, its fullness is yet to come. As we live out the Kingdom now, we do so with the hope of its future fulfillment when Christ returns to establish God's eternal reign. This hope gives us perseverance in the face of hardship and joy in the midst of trial.

A Challenge to Live Differently

As we bring this book to a close, I challenge you to embrace your identity as a citizen of the Kingdom of God. Let the reality of the Kingdom change the way you live, think, and act. The Kingdom demands a response from each of us. Will we live as though we are in a world that is passing away, or will we live as citizens of the Kingdom that is eternal?

In light of all we have discussed, how will you now live? Will you seek first the Kingdom of God and His righteousness (Matthew 6:33)? Will you align your life with the values and mission of the Kingdom, knowing that you are called to be a living expression of God's reign on earth?

The Kingdom of God is not a passive reality; it is active, vibrant, and transformative. As followers of Jesus, we are empowered to be part of the greatest movement the world has ever known. May the truth of the Kingdom continue to shape your life, challenge your thinking, and propel you to live differently, bringing glory to God and advancing His Kingdom on earth.

ABOUT THE AUTHOR

Tom Cornell is the Senior Leader of SOZO Church in Washington state, founder of Walk in the Light International and SOZO Network. Tom is married to his beautiful wife Katy and lives in the Puget Sound area with her and their three kids. He has been in ministry pastoring and teaching the body of Christ since 2008.

He has a passion to see the body of Christ moving from people with an orphan mindset to that of sonship; equipping the body to do the work of Jesus resulting in seeing the Kingdom of God manifested here on earth.

Made in the USA
Columbia, SC
26 February 2025